DISSEMINATING QUALITATIVE RESEARCH IN EDUCATIONAL SETTINGS

DOING QUALITATIVE RESEARCH IN EDUCATIONAL SETTINGS

Series Editor: Pat Sikes

The aim of this series is to provide a range of high-quality introductory research methods texts. Each volume focuses, critically, on one particular methodology, enabling a detailed yet accessible discussion. All of the contributing authors are established researchers with substantial practical experience. While every book has its own unique style, each discusses the historical background of the approach, epistemological issues and appropriate uses. They then go on to describe the operationalization of the approach in educational settings drawing upon specific and vivid examples from the authors' own work. The intention is that readers should come away with a level of understanding that enables them to feel sufficiently confident to undertake their own research as well as critically to evaluate other accounts of research using the approach.

Published titles

Michael Bassey: *Case Study Research in Educational Settings*
Peter Clough: *Narratives and Fictions in Educational Research*
Ivor Goodson and Pat Sikes: *Life History Research in Educational Settings*
Morwenna Griffiths: *Educational Research for Social Justice*
Gary McCulloch and William Richardson: *Historical Research in Educational Settings*
Jenny Ozga: *Policy Research in Educational Settings*
Hilary Radnor: *Researching your Professional Practice*

DISSEMINATING QUALITATIVE RESEARCH IN EDUCATIONAL SETTINGS

A CRITICAL INTRODUCTION

Christina Hughes

Open University Press

Open University Press
McGraw-Hill Education
McGraw-Hill House
Shoppenhangers Road
Maidenhead
Berkshire
England
SL6 2QL

email: enquiries@openup.co.uk
world wide web:www.openup.co.uk

First Published 2003

A catalogue record of this book is available from the British Library

ISBN 0 335 21042 2 (pb)   0 335 21043 0 (hb)

Library of Congress Cataloging-in-Publication Data
CIP data has been applied for

Typeset by RefineCatch Limited, Bungay, Suffolk
Printed in the UK by Bell & Bain Ltd, Glasgow

Contents

Series editor's preface

I had never realized just how fascinating research was in its own right. I was expecting the research methods course to be boring, difficult and all about statistics but I couldn't have been more wrong. There is so much to consider, so many aspects, so many ways of finding out what's going on, and not just one way of representing it too. I have really been surprised.

(Student taking an MA in Educational Studies)

I never knew that there was so much to research. I thought that you just chose a method, applied it, did your statistical sums and came up with your findings. The reality is more complicated but so much more interesting and meaningful.

(Student taking an MA in Educational Studies)

The best thing for me was being told that qualitative research is 'proper' research – providing it's done properly of course. What goes on in schools is so complex and involves so many different perspectives that I think you often need a qualitative approach to begin to get some idea of what's going on.

(Student taking an MA in Sociology)

I really appreciate hearing about other researchers' experiences of doing research. It was quite a revelation when I first became aware that things don't always go as smoothly as some written accounts seem to suggest. It's really reassuring to hear honest reports: they alert you to pitfalls and problems and things that you might not have thought about.

(Doctoral student)

I am sure that comments such as these will be familiar to anyone who has ever taught or taken a course which aims to introduce the range of research approaches available to social scientists in general and those working in educational settings in particular.

The central message that they convey seems to be that the influence of the positivist scientist paradigm is both strong and pervasive, shaping expectations of what constitutes 'proper', 'valid' and 'worthwhile' research. What Barry Troyna wrote in 1994 continues to be the case; namely that:

> There is a view which is already entrenched and circulating widely in the populist circles ... that qualitative research is subjective, value-laden and, therefore, unscientific and invalid, in contrast to quantitative research, which meets the criteria of being objective, value-free, scientific and therefore valid
>
> (Troyna 1994: 9)

Within academic and research circles though, where the development of post-modernist and post-structuralist ideas has affected both thinking and research practice, it can be easy to forget what the popular perspective is. This is because, in these communities, qualitative researchers from the range of theoretical standpoints utilize a variety of methods, approaches, strategies and techniques in the full confidence that their work is rigorous, legitimate and totally justifiable as research. And the process of peer review serves to confirm that confidence.

Recently, however, for those concerned with and involved in research in educational settings, and especially for those engaged in educational research, it seems that the positivist model, using experimental, scientific, quantitative methods, is definitely in the ascendancy once again. Those of us working in England and Wales go into the new millennium with the government-endorsed exhortation to produce evidence-based research which,

> (firstly) demonstrates conclusively that if teachers change their practice from x to y there will be significant and enduring improvement in teaching and learning; and (secondly) has developed an effective method of convincing teachers of the benefits of, and means to, changing from x to y
>
> (Hargreaves 1996: 5)

If it is to realize its commendable aims of school effectiveness and school improvement, research as portrayed here demands 'objectivity', experiments and statistical proofs. There is a problem with this requirement though and the essence of it is that educational institutions and the individuals who are involved in and with them are a heterogeneous bunch with different attributes, abilities, aptitudes, aims, values, perspectives, needs and so on. Furthermore these institutions and individuals are located within complex social contexts with all the implications and influences that this entails. On its own, research whose findings can be expressed in mathematical terms is unlikely to be sophisticated enough to sufficiently accommodate and account for the myriad differences that are involved. As one group of prominent educational researchers have noted:

> We will argue that schooling does have its troubles. However, we maintain that the analysis of the nature and location of these troubles by the school effectiveness research literature, and in turn those writing Department for Employment and Education policy off the back of this research, is oversimplified, misleading and thereby educationally and politically dangerous (notwithstanding claims of honourable intent).
>
> (Slee et al. 1998: 2–3)

There is a need for rigorous research which does not ignore, but rather addresses, the complexity of the various aspects of schools and schooling for research which explores and takes account of different objective experiences and subjective perspectives, and which acknowledges that qualitative information is essential, both in its own right and also in order to make full and proper use of quantitative indicators. The *Doing Qualitative Research in Educational Settings* series of books is based on this fundamental belief. Thus the overall aims of the series are: to illustrate the potential that particular qualitative approaches have for research in educational settings, and to consider some of the practicalities involved and issues that are raised when doing qualitative research so that readers will feel equipped to embark on research of their own.

At this point it is worth noting that qualitative research is difficult to define as it means different things at different times and in different contexts. Having said this Denzin and Lincoln's (2000) generic definition offers a useful starting point:

> Qualitative research is a situated activity that locates the observer in the world. It consists of a set of interpretive practices that make the world visible. These practices transform the world. They turn the world into a series of representations, including field notes, interviews, conversations, photographs, recordings and memos to the self. At this level, qualitative research involves an interpretive, naturalistic approach to its subject matter. This means that qualitative researchers study things in their natural settings, attempting to make sense of, or interpret, phenomena in terms of the meanings people bring to them. Qualitative research involves the studied use and collection of a variety of empirical materials – case study; personal experience; introspection; life story; interview; artefacts; cultural texts and productions; observational, historical, interactional and visual texts – that describe routine and problematic moments and meanings in individuals' lives. Accordingly, qualitative researchers deploy a wide range of interconnected methods, hoping always to get a better fix on the subject matter at hand.
>
> (Denzin and Lincoln 2000: 3)

All of the authors contributing to the series are established, well-known researchers with a wealth of experience on which to draw and all make use of specific and vivid examples from their own and others' work. A consequence of this use of examples is the way in which each writer conveys a sense of research being an intensely satisfying and enjoyable activity, in spite of the specific difficulties that are sometimes encountered.

Disseminating Qualitative Research in Educational Settings: A Critical Introduction is unique in the series insofar as it is an edited collection and because it focuses on an aspect of the research process, rather than on a specific methodology. However, in common with its sister texts it too deals with:

- the historical background of the dissemination of qualitative research;
- epistemological issues;
- ethical issues; and
- appropriate applications.

Guides to research methodologies and methods often present dissemination in a technical, mechanical manner. Descriptions of 'best practice' tend to suggest that there are unproblematic, objective and simplistic approaches and solutions to dissemination issues and situations and assume that audiences will receive and interpret and, where appropriate, act on findings exactly as intended by researchers. On the contrary, Christina Hughes and her contributors demonstrate, through their critical discussions and case studies, that dissemination is an acutely political and ethical process. Whose voices are heard, how findings are re-presented, just exactly what is disseminated and to whom, and how it is interpreted, are crucial concerns. Knowledge is never 'innocent' and sometimes researchers are made extremely conscious of this when they come under pressure to modify, edit, delay or suppress their findings. Whilst such pressure can be, and is, applied to researchers who use quantitative approaches, qualitative researchers also often have to deal with the way in which their work is considered to be anecdotal, biased, lacking in credibility and far too long to be easily read by policy makers. Being required to reduce your work to one side of A4 is, at best, frustrating, and at worst leads to significant distortion and misrepresentation of the voices of both research informants and researchers.

Following on from this last point: to date, a significant gap in the literature that deals with dissemination has been around the personal, subjective and emotional perceptions and experiences of researchers and informants as they relate to dissemination. The case studies presented here all illustrate and reflect on this aspect of dissemination and show how personal involvement and feeling is central to any enactment or understanding of both process and product.

This is an interesting and challenging book. As Series Editor I first read the manuscript over a weekend when I was also involved in teaching research methods to students on a taught doctoral programme. I found that, repeatedly, students were talking about issues and concerns that I had just been reading about. In fact, on a couple of occasions I read from the text in response to points and questions raised in teaching sessions. I think that this is a very telling endorsement indeed!

Final note

It was Barry Troyna who initially came up with the idea for this series. Although his publishing career was extensive, Barry had never been a series editor and, in his inimitable way, was very keen to become one. Whilst he was probably best known for his work in the field of 'race', Barry was getting increasingly interested in issues to do with methodology when he became ill with the cancer that was eventually to kill him. It was during the twelve months of his illness that he and I drew up a proposal and approached potential authors. All of us knew that it was very likely that he would not live to see the series in print but he was adamant that it should go ahead, nonetheless. The series is, therefore, something of a memorial to him and royalties from it will be going to the Radiotherapy Unit at the Walsgrave Hospital in Coventry.

Pat Sikes

References

Denzin, N. and Lincoln, Y. (2000) Introduction: The Discipline and Practice of Qualitative Research, in N. Denzin and Y. Lincoln (eds), *Handbook of Qualitative Research: Second Edition*. California: Sage: 1–28.

Hargreaves, D. (1996) Teaching as a Research-Based Profession: Possibilities and Prospects. TTA Annual Lecture, London TTA.

Slee, R., Weiner, G. with Tomlinson, S. (eds) (1998) Introduction: School Effectiveness for Whom? in *School Effectiveness for Whom? Challenges to the School Effectiveness and School Improvement Movements*. London: Falmer: 1–9.

Troyna, B. (1994) Blind Faith? Empowerment and Educational Research, *International Studies in the Sociology of Education*, 4(1): 3–24.

Acknowledgements

This text began, as I suspect many do, as a response to a problem. As a researcher and academic I had begun to meet with a group of colleagues, Viv Barnes, Lynn Clouder, Judy Purkis and Jackie Prichard, with an interest in, and a concern for, dissemination. We set ourselves up as the 'Aaaagh! Writing Group' (the 'Aaaagh!' conveying our sometime terror at writing for publication) and began as a support group who would share and help develop each other's general research writing. This only happened fairly minimally because, for some reason or another, we thought it would be a good idea to present a conference paper together. This, then, became the focus of our initial meetings. However, as our fields of research traversed the subjects of education, health and social work, we were at first hard pressed to find a topic to which we could all make a contribution. This is because, whilst interdisciplinarity might be lauded in some academic quarters, the practices of academic publication are most usually strongly discipline based. Ironically, therefore, as a group concerned to enhance our dissemination skills and performances, the subject of dissemination became our first focus. In consequence, we presented a conference paper which later led to publication (Barnes et al., 2003).

My work with Viv, Lynn, Judy and Jackie led to a wider interest in research dissemination. With research funding from the Department of Continuing Education at the University of Warwick, I was also very fortunate to secure the research assistance of Arwen Raddon. Arwen undertook, systematically and patiently, a literature review (Raddon, 2001a) and, in so doing, provided an important resource for the development of this text. Whilst this was being conducted, I also contacted colleagues who might, if pressed, contribute to the further development of understandings of dissemination in educational research. This contact, initiated by email, with Meg Maguire, Jane Martin, Tuula Gordon, Loraine Blaxter, Bronwyn Davies, Becky Francis, Carrie Paechter and Chris Mann led to a series of on-line communications which, paradoxically, and owing to the vagaries of networked dissemination, seemed quite often to miss me out of the distribution list! The culmination of these internationally networked conversations led to a symposium on dissemination that was presented at the *Third International Conference of Gender and Education* held at the Institute of Education, University of London, in April 2001. Since that time, and with the support of Pat Sikes, as Commissioning Editor, and Shona Mullen and Anita West at Open University Press, I have been working with Tuula, Bronwyn, Becky, Carrie, Chris and Loraine to produce a text that would challenge conventional wisdom in respect of disseminating qualitative research in educational settings. I believe we have accomplished this.

Of course, each of these wonderful women are not here, in these *Acknowledgements*, to say what it was like working with me and in this they may offer an alternative dissemination story. But for my part, I would say that it has been more than a privilege to work with each of you, as you are the most loving, thoughtful, supportive, creative and intellectually challenging group of people I could have ever chosen to work with.

Christina Hughes
University of Warwick

Contributors' details

Loraine Blaxter is a lecturer in the Institute of Education, University of Warwick. She has extensive anthropological fieldwork experience in the UK, Ireland, France and Papua New Guinea. Her research interests are focused on the impacts of organizational policies and practices on everyday lives and issues of migration and identity. Loraine is an experienced disseminator through teaching, writing and community workshops. In addition to the production of numerous articles and chapters spanning a period of thirty years her publications include the best-selling *How to Research*, 2nd edn. ((2001) Buckingham: Open University Press); *Como Se Hace Una Investigacion* ((2000) Barcelona: Gedisa Editorial); *The Academic Career Handbook* ((1998) Buckingham: Open University Press), each written with Christina Hughes and Malcolm Tight. Loraine serves on the Board of Gender and Education. Loraine is currently engaged in collaborative work concerned with understanding patients as teachers of the doctors of tomorrow.

Bronwyn Davies was born in rural New South Wales and has become internationally well known for her gender research and her poststructuralist writing. She receives frequent invitations to speak about her research in the US, the UK, Europe and Asia. She is a Professor of Education at James Cook University and has published ten books and more than 90 articles and book chapters. Her work has been translated into several languages. She is, in these terms, a practiced and accomplished disseminator. She is at the same time a passionate critic of many of the current principles of dissemination. Her recent publications include a collection of her theoretical writings: *A Body of Writing 1989–1999* (Walnut Creek: Alta Mira Press); a reworking of our understanding of embodied subjecthood: *(In)scribing Body/ Landscape Relations* ((2000) Walnut Creek: Alta Mira Press); a study of preschool children in Japan: *Frogs and Snails and Feminist Tales in Japan* ((forthcoming) Creskill: NJ, Hampton Press, with H. Kasama); and a second edition of *Shards of Glass: Children Reading and Writing Beyond Gendered*

Subjectivities ((2002) Creskill, NJ: Hampton Press). Her outstanding work, *Frogs and Snails and Feminist Tales: Preschool Children and Gender* ((1989) Sydney: Allen and Unwin), has received the Recent Outstanding Book Award from the American Educational Research Association and has been reprinted in several edited collections.

Becky Francis is a Reader in Education and Co-Deputy Director of the Institute for Policy Studies in Education at London Metropolitan University. She has written extensively on gender issues in education, and is one of the editors of the journal *Gender and Education*. Her particular areas of research interest are in the construction of gender identities in education, gender and achievement, and feminist theory. Her recent books include *Boys and Achievement: Addressing the Classroom Issues* ((2000) London: Routledge/Falmer) and the edited collection, *Investigating Gender: Contemporary Perspectives in Education* ((2001) Buckingham: Open University Press, with Christine Skelton).

Tuula Gordon is a fellow of Helsinki Collegium for Advanced Studies, University of Helsinki. Tuula has a wide experience of research and dissemination across Europe and North America. Her research interests are education, young people's transitions, issues of citizenship, nationality and difference and her current research project is 'Becoming a National Citizen: Processes of Differentiation and Diversity. Tuula serves on the boards of *Qualitative Research* and *Gender and Education*. Her publications include *Feminist Mothers* ((1990) London: MacMillan and New York University Press); *Single Women: On the Margins?* ((1990) London: MacMillan and New York University Press); *Making Spaces: Citizenship and Difference in Schools* ((2000) New York: MacMillan and New York University Press, with Janet Holland and Elina Lahlema) and *Ethnographic Research in Educational Settings* (in P. Atkinson et al. *Handbook of Ethnography* (2001) London: Sage, with Janet Holland and Elina Lahlema).

Christina Hughes is a Senior Lecturer in the Department of Sociology, University of Warwick. Her research interests focus on the connections of education, employment and family in women's lives; feminist theory and the development of research methodologies. She serves on the editorial boards of *Gender and Education* and *Gender, Work and Organization* and is founding co-chair of the 'Gender and Education Association'. Her recent publications include *Women's Contemporary Lives: Within and Beyond the Mirror* ((2002) London: Routledge) and *Key Concepts in Feminist Theory and Research* ((2002) London: Sage).

Chris Mann has used a range of research methodologies in social science and social policy research. Substantive areas of research include evaluation of equity initiatives in education (with a particular emphasis on gender), teaching and learning approaches, and differential educational achievement in schools and higher education. She is a visiting fellow at the Oxford Internet Institute and has co-authored a best-selling book which examined the methodological, practical, theoretical and ethical considerations associated with Internet research (Mann, C. and Stewart, F. (2000) *Using the Internet in Qualitative Research: A Handbook for Researching Online*. London: Sage).

Carrie Paechter is a senior lecturer in Education at Goldsmiths College, London. Her research interests, which have been developed out of her previous experience as a mathematics teacher in London secondary schools, include the intersection of gender, power and knowledge, the construction of identity, especially with regard to gender, space and embodiment in and outside schooling, and the processes of curriculum negotiation. She regards herself as a Foucaultian post-structuralist feminist in orientation and writes regularly on issues of research methodology in this context. Her most recent books are *Educating the Other: Gender, Power and Schooling* ((1998) London: Falmer Press) and *Changing School Subjects: Power, Gender and Curriculum* ((2000) Buckingham: Open University Press).

Introduction

Christina Hughes

The research community has not been responsive . . . Its dissemination work has remained mostly incestuous – restricted to the academic community, tempered with the occasional article, speech, seminar or 'vulgarized' book.

(Huberman 1994: 30)

If one reads the literature on dissemination in educational research one could easily be led to believe that some kind of schism exists. This schism seems to rest on a division between practice and theory. On the one hand, researchers are critiqued for not doing enough to spread their ideas beyond their most immediate colleagues. They are seen, therefore, as not embedding dissemination in their research practices. On the other hand, as a literature search would soon demonstrate, there is quite a lot of theorization and discussion about the processes of dissemination.

When it comes to the practices of dissemination, Huberman (op. cit.) is not alone when he castigates the academic research community for neglecting to disseminate ideas and knowledge more widely. Policy makers and government officials in the UK have also been concerned with the perceived lack of systematic dissemination of research knowledge. It is perhaps surprising that this is the case because there is a very strong discourse in the educational research community of paying attention to the needs of 'end users' and practitioners and undertaking research that has relevance for policy and practice. When these features are combined with audit and quality cultures that currently prevail in higher education with their concerns for accountability and value for money one might be forgiven for thinking that a high profile would be given to the dissemination of research. Nevertheless, within both school and continuing education research, dissemination has been seen as particularly problematic. Hillage et al. (1998) identified 'rampant ad-hocery' as the main approach to dissemination in school-based research whilst Schuller (1996) remarks that researchers in adult education have no idea at all how, or if, their ideas are being taken up.

This is not to say that researchers are not interested in developing knowledge about the processes of dissemination. Using the North American educational database ERIC, a key word search under 'dissemination AND research' gave rise to 7096 hits. 13,611 hits were also produced on the same database when using the words 'dissemination AND education'. However, this degree of attention is by no means universal but appears to be primarily a North American phenomenon. For example, a comparison with UK databases suggests something of a geographic divide. Thus, a search within the British Educational Index (BEI) produced a much smaller result. Here, the term 'dissemination' produced 117 hits; 'dissemination AND education' produced 26 hits and 'dissemination AND education research' gave rise to a mere 4 potential sources. Certainly, and regardless of geographical division, as Huberman (op. cit.) suggests much of this work is relatively incestuous. Primarily discussions of dissemination are written by academics for other academics.

Through a wider international focus, this text aims to offer an analysis of dissemination that bridges the gap between a theory-practice divide. It also aims to go beyond an incestuous discussion of dissemination by providing an accessible and up-to-date portrayal of dissemination policies, models and practices in educational settings that is relevant to teachers, administrators, policy makers, students, and, of course, colleagues in higher education. This text is set out in three parts. Part I is comprised of two chapters that explore contemporary policy concerns around dissemination and current models for good practice in dissemination. Part II provides six case studies of dissemination practices, ethics and dilemmas. Part III explores what we can learn from these case studies in order to develop informed practice in the dissemination of qualitative educational research.

Specifically, Chapter 1 explores changing historical and political frameworks of dissemination with particular reference to developments in the UK. This illustrates how 'evidence informed' research and 'national strategies' are key contemporary policy initiatives. Chapter 1 also notes how, through the development of audit trails designed to measure the efficacy of specific research outputs, a concern for dissemination is giving rise to greater attention being given to research impact. Depending upon your perspective, a key implication is, either, further surveillance of the academic research community, or, greater accountability. Within the literature on dissemination, considerable attention has been given to developing models of the dissemination process. This is the focus of Chapter 2, which outlines a series of models that draw on positivist, interpretivist, critical and postmodern understandings of social reality. These two chapters form Part I of this text and as such they provide a summary of contemporary debates and significant models in the field of dissemination.

The focus of Part II is that of the practices and dilemmas of dissemination. Raddon (2001a) indicates how there are a number of diverse strategies and methods of dissemination. These include:

Dissemination through education and training

- continuing education which has been particularly important in the medical field but less so in education (Eraut 1985; Freemantle 1994; Everton et al. 2000);
- in-service training for practitioners (De Landsheere 1982);
- staff development and teacher education (Ben-Peretz 1994).

Dissemination through networks of practitioners, academics and policy makers

- use of/work with an appointed mediating body or agency to disseminate research findings (HEQE 2001; Kirst 2000);
- continuous discussion and interaction with practitioners (Brown 1994; Huberman 1994);
- collaboration and co-operation between researchers and end-users (Ben-Peretz 1994; Hargreaves 1996; Riquarts and Hansen 1998; Kirst 2000);
- identifying networks of leaders and practitioners (Havelock 1969, 1973; Kirst 2000);
- within professional networks (see, for example, the Collaborative Action Research Network (CARN) at www.did.stu.mmu.ac.uk/carn).

Dissemination through the research process

- action and participatory research (Cousins and Simon 1996);
- as an everyday part of qualitative research (Barnes et al. 2003);
- establishing educational research centres responsible for development and dissemination activities (De Landsheere 1982; Geiger 1990).

Dissemination as publishing

- academic activities such as publishing, conferences, networks and lectures (De Landsheere 1982; Blaxter et al. 2001);
- publishing and use of different media (Fauman and Sharp 1958; De Landsheere 1982; Hammersley 2000; Lewando-Hundt 2000).

Aspects of these varied forms of dissemination are present in the series of case studies that are provided in Part II. These have been drawn from eminent educational researchers located in Australia, Norway and the UK.

However, what is distinctive about these case studies is that they have been designed to:

- illuminate how dissemination acts proceed in qualitative research projects; and
- discuss the dilemmas facing qualitative researchers who strive to disseminate their work. These dilemmas include theoretical, ethical, political, emotional and practical issues.

Such a focus is particularly absent in the wider dissemination literature in respect of educational research.

It is common in introductions to edited texts to provide synopses or discussions of such chapters as guidance for the reader. However, I have chosen to leave this until Part III of this text where the focus of concern is to develop informed practice in dissemination. Suffice it to say, readers who would prefer to read a summary of the case studies prior to reading the case studies themselves should, therefore, turn to Chapter 9. Nonetheless, I would highlight the following at this point. First, a significant gap in the literature on dissemination is that of the subjective and emotional realms of human life. All the authors of the case studies reflect on these aspects of dissemination and, in so doing, demonstrate their centrality to an adequate understanding of the meanings and impact of dissemination. Secondly, the case studies offer important reflections on the dilemmas and ethics of dissemination in the light of 'post' epistemological critical thinking. Issues such as 'Who is permitted to speak on behalf of whom?', 'How are we being heard?', 'Who Listens? And Why?' and 'Not Being Heard' are explored in detail. Thirdly, despite the claims of Huberman (op. cit.), and the concerns of politicians and policy makers, these case studies demonstrate a sincere ethical and practical commitment to disseminating research to a wide variety of audiences. Educational researchers are disseminating their work in systematic, thoughtful and creative ways and it is particularly unhelpful to be confronted with discourses that primarily castigate, rather than celebrate, achievements to date. Of course, it may be that (some) educational researchers are not disseminating the kinds of research policy makers and practitioners consider they require and are not disseminating their work in the formats they might also consider desirable. But, that is another matter and is taken up throughout this text.

In addition, I should comment on the order in which the case studies are presented. It is common to read this as representing some kind of hierarchy. Certainly within academic dissemination, the first named author is usually viewed as having made the most significant contribution or has higher status or authority. Authors may therefore assert their ranking on such a basis. Alternatively, researchers attempt to modify such readings by listing authors in alphabetical order. However, the problem with this is that those at the front of the alphabet tend to find themselves more frequently as first named.

There is no designated or pre-set order to the case studies set out in Part II. The order in which they appear is quite random as I selected them by putting each author's name in a hat and pulling them out one by one. I recognize this may do little to change the mores of academic publishing or how status might now be read in the order of authors. But I hope that the very act of stating the case here draws attention to this one aspect of the politics of dissemination.

There is, however, a further aim of this text. This is to develop informed practice in the field of dissemination. In this regard it would be fair to say that the existing literature on dissemination contains a considerable amount of exhortation. This is particularly the case through the development of a series of models (presented in Part I) of the dissemination process where, although there is a recognition of the problematic nature of dissemination, there are also strong messages given about how dissemination should proceed. Such exhortation can also be seen in the various ways in which we are urged to conceptualize dissemination 'correctly'. Academic debate is riven through with contestation over the meanings of key terms (see, for example, Connolly 1993; Tanesini 1994; Hughes 2000a). These debates draw our attention to some important technical and validity issues. They less often focus on the political implications of the more usual claim that a particular meaning of a concept is the only valid one. The implication of this is to license the future use of that particular meaning. This means, as I have commented elsewhere (Hughes 2002a), that contests over meaning are accounts of how terms should be used which, if successful, impact upon future practices, theorization and, of course, the development of appropriate dissemination models.

In this respect, Raddon's (2001a) research into models of dissemination highlights a variety of meanings ascribed to the term dissemination. Each of these compete for dominance as the appropriate way forward. Thus, dissemination has been defined variously as:

The transfer and take-up of knowledge

- the process of implementation in which users 'become aware of, receive, accept and utilise information' (Freemantle et al. 1994: 133);
- the sending *and* receiving of innovations (Barlow et al. 2000);
- a set of rules for the selection of good knowledge (Knott and Wildavsky 1991);
- the transfer or transmission of knowledge from producer to user (Love 1985, cited in Zuzovsky 1994);
- the communication of an innovation (Crosswaite and Curtice 1991);
- mediation between research and practice and between reflection and action (Avalos 1981; Hillage et al. 1998; Seashore Louis 1994).

Intrinsic to the judged performativity of the researcher

- an important element of research performance (Lewando Hundt 2000).

An end-product of research

- a range of activities that take place during the post-writing and assessment stages of research (Blaxter, Hughes and Tight 2001);
- the act of writing up research (McKernan 1991).

A deliberate and managed process that can be contrasted with the free-flow of diffusion

- 'the management of the flow of information, as opposed to diffusion, which leaves the flow of knowledge to a process of "free distribution"' (Stokking 1994: 1549).

This text enters the space that marks exhortation with its worry about how things are and its consequent urging of how they ought to be. It does so with a concern to develop informed practice about dissemination. Informed practice has been chosen in preference to the more common terms of 'best' or 'good' practice. This is because the notion of informed suggests that one knows, or at least has an acquaintance with, the issues and debates that surround dissemination. These debates are conflictual and complex, challenging and thought-provoking. They invoke issues of politics, ethics, representation and subjectivity and draw our attention to competing conceptualizations of social reality. This suggests that, more often than not, there are no simple or easy answers to issues of dissemination. Rather one has to make a critical appraisal of what is possible and what is likely. In this way, the idea of 'informed' contrasts markedly with the tenor of a language that calls upon us to undertake 'good' or 'best' practice. Here, one can be led to believe in easy answers and absolute solutions if only we can follow the ten-point plan. Part III of this text, therefore, has two functions. The first is to draw the text together and to provide a synopsis of the field of dissemination as set out in this text. The second is to take us forward by exploring the areas where further research is warranted in the field of dissemination.

PART I

1 | From dissemination to impact: historical and contemporary issues

Christina Hughes

Introduction

Dear Dr Hughes

<u>Seminar for Educational Journal Editors on 27 November 2000 at the Chamberlain Park Hotel, Alcester Street, Birmingham, B12 0JP</u>

On behalf of the DfEE, ESRC, BERA and UCET, I am pleased to invite you to attend a seminar that we are currently arranging for UK editors of education journals. We envisage that this event will help contribute toward current debates and major current initiatives in educational research.

(Extract from letter sent by the Senior Educational Adviser (Research) Standards and Effectiveness Unit, Department for Education and Employment, dated 9 October 2000)

There is an old truism that there is no such thing as a free lunch. Yet, ostensibly, an invitation sent to editors of UK-based education journals to contribute to current debates, and major current initiatives, in British educational research included not only lunch but coffee and tea as well! Was it too good an opportunity to miss? Certainly the day proved to be illuminating in a number of respects as it enabled participants to discuss contemporary concerns about the future of educational research in a relatively convivial atmosphere. But of primary interest was how, within the rhetoric of quality, practical usefulness, accessibility and participation, issues of research dissemination and impact were riven through the day's discussions. Indeed, the organization and discussion of the day seminar provides an exemplary insight into the changing historical and political frameworks of research dissemination. Duly convened, the day proceeded with some 27 journals represented, together with three publishers, and, of course, the initiators of the invitation.

Through an analysis of this seminar, this chapter provides an account of the growing interest at a national policy level in the United Kingdom in issues of dissemination and impact and, in consequence, what this means for the kind of educational research that will be produced in the future. I begin by outlining the key elements of that interest in terms of what, for many, are perceived to be unjustified attacks on the quality of British educational research. I then turn to a consideration of the broader historical context of the place of research and dissemination within the academy. Here I seek to demonstrate how there has been a change in emphasis in respect of what counts as valued research and, therefore, a change in what kind of research policy makers are requiring to be disseminated. I then explore the implications of these changing values in relation to the above Department for Education and Employment (DfEE) invitation to 'participate' in the development of current initiatives in educational research. In particular, I focus on the work of the National Educational Research Forum (NERF). NERF was established to help achieve the creation of a national strategy that would create a stronger linkage between research, the design and implementation of education policies and the delivery of education in practice. Finally, the chapter illustrates how an interest in dissemination is moving toward the exploration of creating audit trails to measure the impact of research.

Dissemination: a case of 'rampant ad-hocery'?

> The overwhelming impression we gained is one of 'rampant ad-hocery'. There seemed to be little evidence of a comprehensive dissemination strategy by researchers, funders, policy-makers and those acting on behalf of practitioners, and certainly no evidence of a concerted approach.
>
> (Hillage et al. 1998: 36–37)

There has been something of a furore in recent times amongst educational researchers. This rests on three concerning messages that have arisen from reports into the 'quality' of school-based educational research. These messages suggest that educational research tends to be small-scale and qualitative, that there are few reliable or generalizable findings being produced and that not enough account is being taken of existing knowledge. As is well documented, the educational research community has responded to these criticisms in a variety of ways. For example, Lomax (1999) suggests that the educational research community in the UK is facing a crisis of legitimation. Accordingly, she identifies three folk devils whose ideas have spread moral panic (Lomax: 7–10). These are:

- *Michael Barber* as head of the Standards and Effectiveness Unit in the Department for Education and Employment (DfEE). In his book, *The*

Learning Game, Barber sets out a series of proposals for improving the British education system. For example, Barber uses the analogy of the MOT test to argue that teachers need 5-year review of progress reports.

- *David Hargreaves*, who referred to educational research as 'second rate' (Hargreaves 1996). For example, Hargreaves (1997: 405) has commented that 'The core of my original argument is simply stated. It is that educational research should and could have much more relevance for, and impact on, the professional practice of teachers than it now has'. In particular, Hargreaves compared teachers and doctors and referred to them as 'pragmatic professionals who are primarily interested in **what works in what circumstances** and only secondarily in **why** it works' (1997: 410). In consequence, and building on medical models of research, Hargreaves has argued that educational research should be more 'evidence' based.
- *Chris Woodhead*, who wrote in a foreword of a review of the 'quality' of research previously published in four leading educational journals (Tooley with Darby, 1998) that 'Much that is published is, on this [Tooley's] analysis, at best no more than an irrelevance and distraction.'

The responses of the educational research community to these statements have focused on refuting the claims of 'irrelevance', 'bias' and 'low quality'. They have also critiqued evidence-based teaching advocated by Hargreaves (1996, 1997). Davies (1999) describes evidence-based education as operating at two levels. Given that much research already exists, the first level is the use of existing evidence from worldwide research. To achieve this educationalists need to:

- Pose answerable questions.
- Know where and how they can find and retrieve evidence that will help them answer these questions.
- Organize and grade this evidence.
- Determine its relevance to their particular educational needs and contexts.

The second level relates to establishing 'sound evidence where existing evidence is lacking or of a questionable, uncertain, or weak nature' (Davies 1999: 109). In terms of research methodologies, Hargreaves (1997: 412) suggests that 'evidence based teaching is likely to promote much more experimental work than has been undertaken in education in recent years'. Davies comments that the 'objective of evidence based education at this level is to ensure that future research on education meets the criteria of scientific validity, high-quality, and practical relevance that is sometimes lacking in existing evidence on educational activities, processes, and outcomes' (1999: 110). As Davies also points out, the danger of an approach such as that promoted by Hargreaves is that it can 'promote a narrowly utilitarian and philistine approach to research and intellectual life' (1997: 412).

What has been given less of a focus in the debate amongst British educational researchers is the attention that is now being given, at the national policy level, to the dissemination and impact of research. Yet, as Hammersley (2000) notes, 'The dissemination of research findings has been given increasing emphasis in recent years, particularly in the wake of critiques of educational research for failing to have an impact on policymaking and practice'. The relative inattention to dissemination is indeed surprising given, as Ozga (2000) reflects, that this occupied a good proportion of the Hillage Report (Hillage et al. 1998) which itself had its origins in the issues raised by Hargreaves (1996, 1997). Ozga notes that Hillage et al. construct teachers as research recipients who require guidance on the use of research and that:

> ... this contributes to a particular narrative bringing policy, teachers and research together in a seamless web of enlightened practice, in which research appears to drive the action, without prejudice. This is not a story that refers to my earlier narrative of tension between teachers and policy makers, nor does it allow for circumstances where researchers and/or teachers might have different priorities from those of policy makers
>
> (Ozga 2000: 32)

In particular, Hillage et al. (1998: 36–37) identified 'rampant ad-hocery' as the main approach to dissemination. According to the Hillage Report, dissemination was neither conducted systematically nor was there a concerted effort to ensure research was disseminated. The Hillage Report (1998: 37–39 *passim*) identified the following as barriers to dissemination:

- Funders did not necessarily require researchers to submit a dissemination strategy, and where they did, they were often reluctant to fund it properly.
- In some cases, dissemination was not allowed by funders.
- Funding levels often allowed researchers no time to do more than the basic write-up of a project.
- The all important Research Assessment Exercise (RAE) funding system which, despite the written criteria ... was felt to value publication in academic journals at the expense of other media.
- Some of the interviewees from funding bodies felt that many researchers were too busy with their other academic duties to be heavily involved in practitioner dissemination, which was not a valued activity. Some also felt that they did not have the necessary skills.
- Among the practitioner community there were a range of barriers identified, including the impenetrability of much of the language used.
- Teachers have relatively little time available to them to consult research findings.
- Many practitioners thought that the onus did not just lie on them to access research (or for the researchers to directly access users) but that

intermediaries also had responsibilities to target research findings to appropriate audiences and help them interpret the results.
- Is the intended audience in a position to accept what researchers disseminate? If not, how can policy makers assist the dissemination process?

In the UK, the Minister for Education, David Blunkett (2000), took up the issue of dissemination in a speech to a meeting convened by the Economic and Social Research Council (ESRC). The ESRC is the leading funding agency for UK social science research. His comments urged greater contact between users and producers of research:

A recent study conducted by the Science Policy Research Unit (focusing on ESRC's AIDS and Innovation programmes) found that almost all users felt that the most effective way in which social scientists could disseminate their research findings was through direct user engagement in the research projects.

(Blunkett 2000)

He also argued for 'A bolder and more creative approach to accessibility and dissemination'. In this respect, researchers and research funders need to:

- Recognize that effective dissemination is crucial and from the outset consider the different ways in which findings can be communicated. For example, working alongside practitioners to think through the practical implications of research findings can have the greatest impact.
- Communicate interim findings, contribute to ongoing discussions and provide incremental evidence at different stages of the research. This needs to be done carefully. It is often the case that pieces of research dribble out in ways that are embarrassing to researchers and sponsors alike and this can distort the real message.

Finally, in an acknowledgement that current quality regimes for research do not give sufficient credit or status to practitioner-oriented dissemination, Blunkett commented:

We also need to ensure that research accessibility and dissemination are taken into account in the Research Assessment Exercise (RAE). Those who are skilled in making their research accessible – including those who conduct systematic reviews of evidence – must be better recognised and rewarded without compromising on quality. We must reduce the contradictions in what is expected of researchers.

It would seem, therefore, that dissemination is currently high on the public policy agenda. Here the messages that arise from these concerns with dissemination are, of course, related to the more general messages that educational research needs to be accessible and applicable. Educational researchers are being urged to solve 'real' problems of practice through research that is evidence based. Yet, before we explore the contemporary implications of this, it is useful to ask 'How can we understand the furore that surrounded attacks on the present status of educational research as part of a broader shifting relationship between academics and policy makers?'

Historical antecedents

> The university envisaged by Newman is an institution in which conversations of a certain sort – about truth, beauty and goodness – will not simply be **possible**. Such conversations are always possible, even, one is almost tempted to say, in present-day universities. In Newman's university, though, conditions will be such as to **foster** such conversations, and the conversations will be between those disciplined and expert in the various central fields of human knowledge, and between people aiming to become so disciplined and expert. Academic freedom, envisaged as the freedom to teach and research, is crucial to those teaching in such an institution because they will otherwise be subject to pressures which will take them away from their central task, particularly the pressures to specialize narrowly and to serve various short-term ends, economic and political.
>
> (Tight 1988: 11, emphasis in original)

Tight's (op. cit.) analysis of the idea of the university as a 'special type of institution, with special duties and values' (Tight 1988: 6) draws particularly on the vision forwarded by Cardinal John Henry Newman (1801–1890). Born in London and writing in the second half of the nineteenth century, Newman idealized the notion of the university as a place free from direct concerns with practical purposes and social relevance. For Newman, academic freedom meant that the university was a place for conversation and speculation. However, writing in the late 1980s, Tight notes how the notion of academic freedom as the relative freedom of choice in what one researches and teaches had become more of an issue than at any time since the student disturbances of the 1960s. Cutbacks in state funding, the impact of voluntary and compulsory redundancies, the growth of short-term contract working and alleged suppression or abuse of 'free speech' are cited as the main reasons for this. In particular, Tight comments on the 'stultifying consequences of central direction and control of academic life' (1988: 2). This appears an apt phrase to convey the direction in which the relationship between academic and policy maker is shifting in terms of research output. What we can witness is a move away from a view of research as scholarly activity pursued mainly for the development of a field of knowledge and for an audience of colleague academics. It is a move towards a view of educational research as a public resource that should be pursued only if it has a perceived outcome in terms of the development of practices.

There has, historically, been a series of strong divisions within academic life between the 'pure' and 'applied' sciences; the scholar and the technician or practitioner; and research for self-enlightenment and research for the development of a technology that has a direct use (Hargreaves, 1999). In such a culture, academic research has been primarily viewed as the training ground for an academic career that is driven by the need to create bodies of leading-edge knowledge in finite fields of study. It has not been viewed as a route to producing guides to action. Similarly, dissemination was primarily seen as publication by academics for the academic community and served, as it still does today, an important role in career advancement. In such a model there needs to be no direct intention of application to what are euphemistically called 'real world' problems. For example, Sax (1979: 1) remarks that for centuries 'common sense, authority, intuition, revelation or logic' was seen as better placed than scientific knowledge to provide answers to educational problems.

To a certain extent such an analysis of these kinds of divisions can be best understood as a useful heuristic device. As such it enables one to explain, and explore, the values, power issues and relative status of different forms of academic work, and academic workers, rather than to portray an accurate representation of the whole corpus of the academic community. For example, the division between 'pure' and 'applied' research can be seen as one of status with the former, usually, occupying the higher ground of privilege and stature. Nonetheless, there were exceptions to this model with a number of social researchers engaged in dissemination in the policy arena. For example, Fabians such as Beatrice and Sydney Webb in the late nineteenth and early twentieth centuries were engaged in publishing, lobbying and policy making as a means of disseminating their research and attempting to bring about social change.

Nevertheless, it was particularly during, and following, World War II that governments of Western nations specifically began to demand a new type of knowledge that would 'assist in national decision-making by enlightened policy makers' (OECD 1995: 39). Weiss (1977) notes that there was a marked shift towards the use of data in government planning and a call for solutions to 'real world' problems. She comments that:

> There was much hoopla about the rationality that social science would bring to the untidy world of government. It would provide hard data for planning, evidence of need and of resources. It would give cause-and-effect theories for policy making, so that statesmen [sic] would know which variables to alter in order to effect the desired outcomes.
>
> (Weiss 1977: 4)

Within the field of education, this entailed a move towards 'decision-oriented or applied educational research' (OECD 1995: 39). In addition, social science was increasingly recognized as funded by, and therefore needing to serve the needs of, society as a whole (Fauman and Sharp 1958). Researchers were urged to disseminate knowledge on the widest possible level and to ensure that those groups to whom their research would be useful were made aware of its existence. In consequence, and as part of the drive for the development and dissemination of applied research, the 1960s and 1970s saw an unprecedented worldwide growth of government-led public and private research centres and institutions. This not only enabled universities to respond to social needs, it also contributed to the global dissemination, and some would say hegemony, of US-based research knowledge (Geiger 1990; Stahler and Tash 1994).

Notwithstanding this interest and funding in applied research, we have to wait until the 1970s before we see research being undertaken into the topic of dissemination itself in the field of education. Here Stokking (1994) notes that education lags behind the health and agriculture fields where a focus on practice has been historically stronger. In addition, the research that has been conducted has focused primarily on schooling rather than the broader fields of lifelong and adult continuing or further and higher education (see, for example, Rudduck and Kelly 1976; Schuller 1996; Hillage et al. 1998). Raddon (2001a) notes that by dealing systematically with the dissemination of empirical evidence in education it was increasingly believed that practice would improve as had been the case in industry, agriculture and health care. For example, Weiss (1982) comments on how, in the late 1970s and early 1980s in primary and secondary education, there was a growing interest in identifying 'what works' and in eradicating what did not.

In addition, over the 1970s, 1980s and 1990s, there have been strong critiques made of educational researchers and policy makers in terms of their respective roles in the dissemination process. Although, to say the least, the interest by governments in academic research has been by no means a straightforward story of unmitigated support, there has continued to be the argument that dissemination beyond the academic community has been largely overlooked in educational research. Indeed, despite academics' involvement in areas such as community work and consulting, Paulsen and Feldman (1995) note that the service element of scholarship has been omit- . ted from what they describe as a very static understanding of the role and value of scholarship. On the other hand, researchers repeatedly express concerns about the under-utilization of research knowledge by educational policy makers, planners, administrators and practitioners. This has led to what Weiss (1977) describes as a two-fold job. That is 'to see that social science knowledge produced is relevant to government and to transfer that knowledge to decision makers in ways that enhance their capacity to use it' (Weiss 1977: 6).

There are three main consequences of these debates. First, it has meant that one of the major concerns in the literature has been a focus on exploring issues of knowledge transfer in order to increase the efficiency and effectiveness of dissemination activities. This has led to the development of a series of models that span the positivist, interpretivist and critical paradigms of social research (see Chapter 2 for a further discussion). Secondly the desire to close the gap, so to speak, between knowledge produced and knowledge used has also led to greater calls, from a variety of political persuasions, for educational researchers to increase their dissemination activities (Hammersley 2000) and to form linkages between research, policy and practice (Mahony 1994; Hillage et al. 1998; Ginsburg et al. 2000; Kirst 2000; Ozga 2000). Such linkages, it is argued, would not only enhance communication between various groups but would also take researchers out of their ivory towers and bring them closer to the 'real' concerns of practitioners and policy makers. Raddon (2001a) notes that it is perhaps not unrelated that this call for increased dissemination of evidence and research-based practice has come at the same time as a drive towards a knowledge-based economy. Where knowledge is viewed as a more vital economic resource than either capital or labour, it is inevitably seen to play a key role in the economic development and continued competitiveness of universities and nations. Indeed, there is a growing body of literature on university-industry linkages, with a dedicated journal *Industry and Higher Education*, with dissemination central to the entrepreneurship and competitiveness of universities worldwide (Bird and Allen 1989). Thirdly, the issue of relevancy is primarily translated as the production of knowledge that has a practical, daily use in the classroom. This is what is perceived to be 'relevant' knowledge. Here there appears to be a strong desire for research to produce a form of knowledge that is readily understandable and quick to apply to complex problems in the social world. As Chapter 2 demonstrates there is a growing awareness in the more critical literature that dissemination is not a politically neutral activity. Moreover, as Chapters 2 and 9 also explore, we cannot rule out complex ontological and epistemological issues at the heart of dissemination activities in terms of what can be known and how we might know. However, the prioritization of the economic over the social aspects of education has led to an emphasis of governments and policy makers seemingly requiring researchers to make 'simple statements about complex issues' (Ozga 2000: 81) that can be disseminated and applied countrywide.

It is at this point that we should return to our 'free lunch' seminar. Here the rationale appears to be that if research is to be 'useful' in the ways currently prescribed then researchers and funders need to be more aware of good practices of dissemination. Journal editors are seen as key gatekeepers in the dissemination chain. Thus, with a concern for a systematization of research and dissemination, it would appear to be logical to invite editors to 'participate' in the development of dissemination strategies that are more directly linked to national policy concerns. Indeed, the DfEE letter to editors noted how academic journals play a crucial role in the dissemination of research findings. However, as I seek to demonstrate, the concern that surrounds dissemination is more accurately to be understood in terms of impact.

The seminar agenda: a personal perspective

> How should such an initiative [a Research and Development Strategy for Education] be taken forward without delay to produce agreed quality criteria to inform the Forum's strategy? How can we ensure that agreed quality criteria are applied by researchers, funders, journal editors and others?
>
> (The National Educational Research Forum: A National
> Strategy Consultation Paper 2000: 7)

The design of the day was a mixture of presentations and discussions. The presentations were focused on the National Educational Research Forum (NERF), the DfEE-funded Evidence for Policy and Practice (EPPI) Centre based at the Social Science Research Unit, Institute of Education, University of London (see Oakley 2002 for a discussion of the evidence-based work of the EPPI centre) and the ESRC-funded Teaching and Learning Programme. The discussions were undertaken with the whole group during the morning and with smaller groups during the afternoon. In this sense, therefore, there appeared to be a concern to set out the current policy framework in terms of information-giving about NERF, the EPPI Centre and the Teaching and Learning Programme. Notwithstanding, as I shall discuss below, the concern was also about how to improve the impact of research through various forms of dissemination. In addition, there was a concern to assess the feasibility, and views, of journal editors in terms of coming to some kind of agreement about the criteria that would be applied to assessing the validity of papers for publication. Overall, my notes indicate that there were three primary objectives that the organizers had set themselves:

- To explore the possibilities for improving communication between journal editors, DfEE, NERF, EPPI Centre, and the ESRC Teaching and Learning Programme.
- How can we ensure that researchers, funders, journal editors and others create a set of agreed [i.e. uniform] quality criteria?
- Discuss the possible implications of evidence-informed practice and policy in respect of the development of educational research.

The discussion during the morning was more fully focused on the role of journals and the issue of quality criteria and it is this discussion that I shall also focus on here. Suffice it to say that the afternoon sessions were far more organic in their concerns than those that the formal agenda indicate. Primarily the focus of the morning debate was in terms of the readability, usability and accessibility of academic journals for practising teachers. Such a focus begs a presumption that writing for teachers is a primary, even the only, purpose of academic research. As we have seen above, this is not necessarily the case. On the one hand, it is a highly disputable objective in terms of the purpose of the university as a place that should foster critical, independent, intellectual judgement. On the other hand, the career systems of university life reward those who publish in high-ranking journals that by and large are not designed to be read by practitioners. In this regard my notes indicate that the idea of a divide between academics and practitioners/policy makers was replicated in the questions that were raised. For example, participants asked:

- 'Who is the audience for journals?'
- 'Is there a practice-theory divide in the audiences?'
- 'Do teachers, users, policy makers read journals?'
- 'Should academic journals be read by practitioners?'

Nonetheless, in the main, there was a considerable amount of sympathy for academic research to inform teaching practices in schools. Indeed, one member of the audience commented on the direct usefulness of research to developing practice in terms that: *'If you are not doing research to improve practice why are you doing it?'*

As we might expect, the responses to these questions were varied and critically informed. One publisher reflected on the impact of technology on the dissemination of knowledge to point out that Internet access had highlighted how it was the accessibility of individual articles that was important rather than the whole journal. Others raised points about keeping an international perspective to the debate, that education was not simply a concern of schools but was highly relevant in non-school environments and that one of the roles of journals was to keep on the agenda issues that might have fallen off. Overall, however, as one participant noted, the discussion replicated divisions between teachers and researchers and a great concern with accessible knowledge. As he noted in this respect, 'The most common word in the discussion is "accessible".'

Given the contemporary policy environment, it is no surprise that the formal steer in the agenda appeared to be toward the publication of what is perceived to be practically useful research and that authors should write in 'plain [sic] English'. Indeed, as one participant commented 'Classroom teachers haven't got a lot of time. They want straightforward language.' Such a view confirms the views presented in the Hillage Report (1998: 35) that journal publications 'lack an element of "user-friendliness" in either [their] scope or presentation as far as practitioners are concerned'. For example, one respondent is quoted in the Hillage Report as follows:

A lot of it is stodgy, pedantic nonsense and some of it is really good. Much is very esoteric, looks at a very specific area that is of marginal interest, statistically laden and can't draw conclusions that impact on practice.

(Hillage et al. 1998: 35)

Lest we believe that this is primarily a concern for teacher education, those in the broader field of lifelong learning have similarly taken up the accessible and practical banner for educational research. Thus, Lavender (2000: 7) comments that research should:

• Result in summaries in plain English;
• Offer usable data to practitioners;
• Be accessible in location and language;
• Directly impact on practice;
• Be in response to practice.

With regard to the role of journal editors in this process, the exhortation that we might all come to an agreement with regard to the 'quality' criteria that would apply to publication is an interesting one. It certainly confirms the view of McIntyre and Wickert (2000: 160) that 'a rationalist model of policy analysis continues to dominate in research and policy discourses' and this model is one of linear direction. It also confirms Ozga's (2000: 32) view that there are widespread assumptions that 'there is a "top-down" flow of energy and ideas that produces planned outcomes and that "evidence" will produce consensus in practice'. It further confirms the view that 'quality' is the new imperialism of educational research and implies, despite evidence to the contrary, that all journals are of an equal standard and, indeed, have an equal standing. Moreover, it completely ignores the international nature of many journals and the implications this has for what is published and what is seen to be relevant. In addition, the notion of coming to agreement presupposes 'agreement', albeit implicit and partial at the level of everyday cultural practice, does not already exist. As Weiner (1998) notes through an analysis of an ESRC-funded 'Getting Published Project' that looked at the practices of journal editorial boards in education, psychology and sociology:

> There was consensus among editors regarding the role and responsi-bilities of editors and editorial boards – which was to take main policy decisions on which manuscripts to publish so as to provide up-to-date thinking and 'cutting edge' research in a particular field or discip-line. . . . Other areas of agreement included: how referees were chosen (mainly through personal and professional networks); criteria for assessment of manuscripts (clarity of exposition and writing, original-ity, and relevance to the field); feedback to authors (a copy of the referees' reports plus a covering letter from the editor); and use of 'blind' refereeing system (removal of author's name).

> (Weiner 1998: 8)

It has to be said that there was disagreement amongst those present at the DfEE seminar with the view that there could be agreed criteria for publication. The reasons for this relate to a critique of the idea that all research should be accessible and practical and the need to maintain diverse journals for diverse needs and cultures. For example, one participant pointed out that he would like to insert the word 'obscurity' into the debate in order to highlight how the desire for agreement 'Obscures rather than clarifies the political dimensions of research.' In particular, it obscured the issue that the criteria that were being promoted were those related to positivistic, large-scale studies and that 'If you are going to start imposing these criteria you are going to put off practitioner research.' This participant also critiqued the idea that the complexities of the social world could be made easily and readily accessible in a short journal article. In this respect, he sought to bring into the debate the idea that new, innovative ideas can often be challenging and problematic by saying that 'If you are going to do something new you need difficulty.'

Beyond dissemination to impact

> How can existing experience in education and other sectors be drawn upon to construct an 'impact' model for research and development in education? . . . It is the Forum's view that research and development intended to have an impact needs to be designed and funded with in-built measures of impact included from the outset.
> (The National Educational Research Forum: A National Strategy Consultation Paper 2000: 9)

A NERF sub-group report (NERF, 2000) draws a distinction between dissemination and impact. The report notes that dissemination is the most common term and refers to the spreading of awareness of research findings to those outside the research team. Impact refers to the influence or effect that the research has on its audiences. As the report points out, a piece of research may be very effectively disseminated in terms that it is well known. However, dissemination is no guarantee of changes in practice.

The report identifies five potential communities who have an interest in research impact. These are funders, researchers, policy makers, practitioners and the media. It also notes that much research assumes an implicit model of research impact. This is one of a linear direction from researcher to practitioner and/or policy maker. The report notes that this is an erroneous conception of the process and argues for understandings to be based on a more interactive model of relationships between researchers, practitioners and policy makers. The report calls for the development of greater knowledge with regard to a number of issues in relation to impact. These relate to analyses of successful knowledge transfer and effective application. The report concludes with a number of questions, one of which is concerned with the development of impact trails and measurements that would lead to maximizing positive impact.

The organizers of the DfEE seminar were certainly concerned with issues of impact. For example, one presentation during the morning was focused on the efficacy of television for getting the message across in an accessible way and there was much talk about computer-mediated communication and information technologies. For the many educational researchers who have worked closely with a number of different groups, and who work within more participatory research paradigms, the exhortation to use visual media is rather like teaching the proverbial granny to suck eggs. One such example is that of Slim and Thompson (1993) who illustrate how story-telling, theatre and puppets are effective methods of dissemination.

There are, of course, a variety of responses to this concern with impact. A greater knowledge and understanding of the processes associated with impact may indeed enhance the relevance and usefulness of social science research. Certainly, there are also several intellectual challenges in developing such understandings. Of itself, therefore, the study of impact may prove to be an interesting and fruitful field of research endeavour. However, current concerns with impact, and of course with dissemination, need to be contextualized within the policy framework of a proposed national strategy that is at the centre of NERF's remit. As the British Educational Research Association's (BERA) responses to NERF have highlighted, 'educational research must not be too firmly hitched to government' (BERA 1998). In particular, this agenda is one that, as we have seen, has a considerable focus on practical applications. David Blunkett (2000) sums this up as follows:

> We're not interested in worthless correlations based on small samples from which it is impossible to draw generalisable conclusions. We welcome studies which combine large scale, quantitative information on effect sizes which will allow us to generalise, with in-depth case studies which provide insights into how processes work.
>
> (Blunkett 2000)

The connection between national strategies for evidence-informed, practically focused research and research funding has consequent implications for academic careers and employability. In addition, should the audit culture extend its frame of reference to include the measurement of impact, the funding regime will further constrain the options in favour of research that promises to solve fairly narrowly defined practice-based issues. The proposed move towards large-scale, evidence-based research is simultaneously a move towards larger, and fewer, dedicated research centres. This, of course, restricts the opportunities for a widespread engagement in funded research by members of the academy and practitioner researchers. In addition, large-scale, quantitative research is not the only paradigm of educational research, yet such a model leaves qualitative researchers with a limitation of choice if they wish to continue to receive funding for their work. For example, they might move much more fully towards mixed-methodological approaches (cf. Blunkett's call for 'case studies to explore processes') through a combination of quantitative and qualitative designs. Yet it is not impossible to envisage the inherent difficulties of acquiring funding for more open-ended forms of qualitative research where researchers work within flexible research designs and strive for a grounded theorization that seeks to capture the unexpected and unanticipated. 'What works?' might be an outcome of such research, but it could not be guaranteed at the outset of the design. Indeed, in his discussion of the value of evidence-based research, Hargreaves (1997: 412) comments that whilst he believes in a plurality of research approaches nevertheless 'ethnography . . . may not be in the vanguard here'. What future is this for the qualitative researcher?

Summary

This chapter was based on an invitation to a 'free lunch' in order to participate in discussions that will inform the future of educational research in the UK. Accordingly, I have outlined the contemporary policy environment, and its historical antecedents, in respect of the dissemination of qualitative research. I have indicated how there is a strong move towards evidence-informed approaches that focus on a 'What works?' model of the purposes of research. This suggests that whilst there is much talk concerned with encouraging researchers to disseminate their work more widely, and more systematically, it is practical impact that is going to be a key criterion for evaluating research. Certainly, there is a place, and a case, for this kind of work. However, what is of concern is that this should be the primary, and perhaps the only, kind of research that is deemed appropriate for informing policy and practice debates and for which funding will ultimately be available. Such a monochromatic view is certainly being challenged within the educational community. In this regard, we might say that, whilst there may be no such thing as a 'free lunch', it does not mean that we have to eat everything that is put on the plate before us.

2 | Models of dissemination
Christina Hughes

Introduction

There is a children's nursery school about five miles from where I live called 'The Sojourner Truth Day Nursery'. Sojourner Truth was born into slavery in late eighteenth-century North America. When slavery was abolished Sojourner became a travelling preacher. She is most famous for her speech 'Ain't I a Woman', in which she made a powerful connection between the plight of slaves, issues of 'race' and womanhood. To see her name being taken up in what is predominantly a white, middle-class area that is hardly noted for its radicalism begs an important question. Is this a case of systematic dissemination whereby ideas are carefully planted, nurtured and come to fruition? Or is the naming of this nursery the result of a more widespread diffusion where ideas are scattered haphazardly and lie there waiting to be picked up or ignored?

I raise these questions because I think they indicate something of the problematic nature of dissemination. This is the issue of definition. As we shall see, in seeking to define dissemination, and therefore to develop models of the dissemination process, there is a tension that the metaphors of planting and scattering convey. On the one hand, there are those who seek to discriminate between the processes of dissemination and diffusion by asserting that dissemination is a systematic process and diffusion is more haphazard. On the other hand there is a recognition that it is not possible to exert absolute control over whether, or how, ideas and practices are taken up.

This tension, between seeking to exert control and at the same time recognizing the host of meanings, personal investments, the problematics of communication and the politics of social research, is evident in the variety of models of dissemination discussed in this chapter. In this respect, there are three intertwined features of research that have impacted on the development of dissemination models. First, these models demonstrate how issues of ontology and epistemology are significant. Thus, there are models based on more positivist conceptions of dissemination through to interpretivist and critical views. As the case studies in this text indicate, those with interests in dissemination have also considered the impact of postmodernism and poststructuralism.

Secondly, different research designs give rise to a differential place for dissemination. As research methods textbooks will testify, both qualitative and quantitative research designs tend to view dissemination as an end point to field or survey work. The case studies in this text actually challenge this view in respect of qualitative research. Because of the closeness that qualitative research designs require between researcher and respondent, these case studies demonstrate how dissemination is part of the everyday of qualitative research. Nevertheless, in terms of formal design, we need to look towards those who undertake more participatory forms of research to find recognition that dissemination is an integral part of the research process. For example, through the ways that the beneficiaries of the proposed research are integrated into the design, collection and analyses stages of the research, Participatory Action Research designs view dissemination as integral to the whole process. Action Research models also include dissemination as part of the evaluative cycle of ongoing action.

Thirdly, and relatedly, different ethical models concerned with the purposes of research have their impact. For example, for those researchers with concerns for social justice and who work within critical models of social research, issues of power will be highly significant. Here, considerable emphasis is given to developing praxis or bringing about political social change. In this respect, attention to what is disseminated cannot be separated from how it is disseminated. Again this is a key theme of many of the case studies. In contrast, the ethical position at the heart of positivist dissemination models assumes a more benign view of the social agent who will recognize, as self-evident, the worth of innovations. In such a model, the power dimensions between expert and recipient do not come under scrutiny.

This chapter explores these issues through a series of models that can be found in the literature. These models draw, respectively, on positivist, revised modernist, interpretivist, evidence-based, critical and deconstructive views of dissemination. They demonstrate the inter-relationship of ontological, epistemological and ethical perspectives central to research design and dissemination procedures.

The heritage of positivism

Traditional models of dissemination have primarily been located within positivist frameworks. At a general level, positivism proceeds within the view that social science research should mirror, as near as possible, procedures of the natural sciences. The research should be objective and detached from the objects of research and it is considered possible to capture, through research instruments, 'real' reality (Guba and Lincoln 1994). In dissemination terms, a positivist framework assumes that

> well-developed, research-based innovations will spread within defined populations of users thereby reducing the gap between what we know (according to knowledge producers or researchers) and what we do (defined by the action of knowledge users or practitioners)
>
> (Cousins and Simon 1996: 200)

As an adjunct to this, the view of human behaviour in such models appears to rest on a combination of the rational agent and humanistic beneficence. Thus, rational and well-meaning individuals will recognize and take up 'good' knowledge in a progressive and enlightening way.

Research Development and Diffusion Model (RD&D)

The classic example of such an approach is that of the *Research, Development and Diffusion Model*. This presents the dissemination process as systematic, rational and linear, moving from basic to applied research and development, and then on to mass dissemination (Havelock 1973). It is perhaps the most conventional and standardized view of dissemination. This model contains extensive planning and high levels of investment because of 'anticipated long-term benefits in *efficiency* and *quality* of the innovation and its suitability for *mass audience dissemination*' (Havelock 1973: 161, emphasis in original). It has been particularly influential in industry, space, defence and agriculture and assumes that knowledge is not necessarily produced to meet a previously identified need but may well be produced for its own sake. Within such a view utilization will occur because 'if the knowledge is there, a user will be found for it' (Havelock 1969: 41).

Resting within the scientific, positivist paradigm and Enlightenment tradition, this top-down, expert-driven model portrays the end user or 'mass audience' as passive and rational. It also portrays dissemination as a relatively unproblematic, and indeed relatively benign, concept. This is because it suggests that 'good', 'expert' knowledge can be packaged for delivery to users who will recognize its benefits and accept it as effective and safe (McMillan and Schumacher 1986; Marsh 1986; Cousins and Simon 1996).

The Cascade Model

Bearing many of the positivistic, expert-led hallmarks of the RD&D model, a second example is that of the *Cascade Model*. McDevitt (1998: 425) indicates that the notion of cascading knowledge down a chain of command 'works on the principle that a small team of trainers will train a larger group, who will in turn pass on their knowledge and skills to a further group'. McDevitt offers an analysis of the cascade model through a review of in-service teacher training in Botswana. A key perceived advantage of the cascade model is that large numbers of teachers can be trained in new techniques in a relatively short period of time. In Botswana 1000 teachers received training in intensive two- or three-day workshops. In this respect, McDevitt notes that the cascade model is relatively economical as one main learning package is produced and replicated for each audience.

However, McDevitt notes a number of problems with this model. For example, the key beneficiaries of the project were the project facilitators rather than the teachers. This was because knowledge and understanding was more highly developed by facilitators through the processes of teaching others. In addition, the one-way transmission process within this one-for-all model means that review and refinement are not easily accommodated. Thus, it proved difficult to change the process in the light of difficulties in respect of mixed ability groups and concerns that as knowledge was passed down the cascade there was a danger of it being distorted. McDevitt comments that perhaps the failure of the model 'lies within the metaphor of the cascade itself: if you're too far away from the source, you can easily avoid getting soaked' (1998: 428).

Revised modernist models of dissemination

There are a number of criticisms that are made of positivist models of dissemination. These include the front-loading nature of the model in that more emphasis is given to the development of knowledge and much less attention is paid to how knowledge is disseminated and diffused. Linear models also tend to portray knowledge as something like a parcel that can be passed from one individual to another. This knowledge is assumed to remain intact in the process of transfer. These criticisms have led to much more emphasis being given to the complexity of linkages, and contextual features, existing between the producers and users of knowledge in the development of dissemination models. In this respect Cousins and Simon note that a blending of social constructivism and positivism is central to contemporary models of dissemination operating within the policy arena. What is significant to such models is the view that 'information is communicated, transmitted, or otherwise picked up, and it becomes usable knowledge only when cognitively processed by the user' (Cousins and Simon 1996: 200). However, Cousins and Simon also note that policy models do not accept a more extreme interpretivist view that the interpretations of one group or individual cannot be seen as more valid than another's. This means that models of dissemination in the policy arena can be described as resting on revised modernist perspectives. Here it is important to recognize that knowledge will only be taken up if it appears relevant and useful to a potential recipient. It is, therefore, the job of the disseminator to make that relevance explicit. However, such a model does not give up on a view of knowledge as potentially enlightening and leading to better practice. It also does not challenge the power of the expert. The following offers one example of this approach.

Funder-specific models

Government departments' and research funders' concerns about the dissemination and utilization of knowledge have led to a number of good practice guides being developed by specific agencies. Such guides can clearly be an aid to potential researchers as they highlight policy priorities or outline expectations about how dissemination might proceed. As an example of this form of dissemination model, the following is drawn from the UK Government's Department for Education and Employment's Higher Education: Quality and Employability Division (HEQE 2001).

HEQE fund a small number of projects that are concerned to strengthen the relevance of higher education to the world of work. As a requirement of funding, HEQE expects each project to have a dissemination strategy. This is because 'dissemination is not just a matter of distributing materials or presenting reports to conferences. Its purpose is to ensure that relevant audiences understand what was done and how they might use the lessons to meet their own needs' (HEQE 2001). The HEQE guide offers advice on such issues as how to make your research relevant to potential audiences. For example, they suggest that

> Employers are more likely to be influenced by the concrete experience of trusted colleagues than by academic studies. The opportunity to meet other employers who have benefited, or to hear from individual participants is more likely to make an impact than presentations from academics. Do you have good stories to tell of how your project impacted on particular employers?
>
> (HEQE 2001)

In addition, the guide stresses that there is no single dissemination strategy as this varies in terms of topic and audience. However, they suggest that all strategies should address the following questions:

- Who are the audiences for your dissemination?
- What will you want them to understand?
- What action might they take as a result?
- How does the project relate to users' interests, circumstances and current understanding?
- What approaches to dissemination are planned, how and when?

In addition HEQE set out eleven guiding principles for dissemination:

- *Talk to all relevant audiences* because change usually arises through a combination of 'top-down' and 'bottom-up' strategies.
- *Focus on your audience's problems* to enhance the relevancy of your work.
- *Engage your audience* through workshops and participatory activities rather than relying on print or lectures.
- *Choose appropriate modes* of dissemination for your audience and purpose. For example, publishing in a refereed journal is more likely to influence an academic audience.
- *Explain the policy context* as this enables audiences to see how the project fits into a larger picture. HEQE comment that they can facilitate access to relevant prestigious speakers who can undertake this task.
- *Explain the development context* in order that your audience has a sense of how it fits in with past development work. Again HEQE suggest they can put project holders in touch with relevant speakers.
- *Include previous work* in order to illustrate how your project contributes to what is already known.
- *Disseminate from the start* as this can strengthen interest and the consequent building of collaborative networks.
- *Make full use of existing channels* such as newsletters, meetings of professional bodies, items on the agenda of staff groups and so forth as this is more economical and builds credibility with your audience.
- *Avoid duplication* with projects in similar areas as this will confuse your audience and is wasteful.
- *Evaluation and monitoring* of dissemination activities enables you to know how your work is being received and understood.

This model can be understood in terms of a 'normative-reductive' strategy (Marsh 1986) through which disseminators seek to manipulate recipients' perceptions of an innovation by identifying and gaining the support of influential groups, and individuals, and by using strategies that worked with other innovations. It also bears many of the hallmarks of what Havelock (1969) has termed the social interaction model. Key features of this model include the constant analysis of the processes of dissemination by, for example, researchers identifying:

- The characteristics of innovations that are most likely to be adopted.
- The networks and opinion leaders who might influence their take-up.
- Those individuals or groups most likely to adopt innovations.
- The steps through which an innovation goes from conception to use.

These are, of course, central features of the HEQE model. Havelock suggests that this model eschews an understanding of society that is 'systemic' and working towards one common goal. Rather, it assumes society is made up of complex networks of roles, communications, associations and barriers, each of which are operating at different levels. Thus, researchers evaluate the flow of dissemination and the impact of social relations, formal and informal networks, the social position of users, group identity, and culture on the outcomes of the dissemination process (Katz et al. 1963; Havelock 1969; Raddon 2001a) with a view, clearly, to enhance take-up.

Sustained interactivity: a classic interpretivist model of dissemination

An interpretivist approach 'looks for culturally derived and historically situated interpretations of the social life-world' (Crotty 1998: 67). Although interpretivism has many variants, such as hermeneutics, phenomenology and symbolic interactionism, it is, more generally, viewed as central to qualitative approaches to research. Here, as Ely et al. (1991) note, the focus is on studying individuals or groups in their natural settings because events can only be understood adequately if they are seen in context. In addition, qualitative research is an interactive process through which the people studied teach the researcher about their lives.

This view of interpretivism and the conduct of social research would appear central to Huberman's model of sustained interactivity. Huberman (1994) is concerned to bridge the academic–practitioner gap. This leads him to argue that 'interpersonal links, spread through the life of a given study, are the key to research use' (Huberman 1996: 22). This is because reciprocal conversations develop which enable practitioners to express their concerns in respect of how the study will affect them. These conversations also enable researchers to respond by reframing aspects of their study. As Huberman comments this is 'something that seldom happens when a completed piece of research is "handed off" to audiences' (1994: 22). Nevertheless, Huberman's model does not promote a *laissez-faire* approach through which findings will be diffused in the everyday of research. Rather, he argues that sustained interactivity requires dissemination competence and intermediaries.

Dissemination competence involves 'putting out different products for distinct audiences, multiple channels (visual, in print), redundancy of the important messages that researchers want to get across, in-person contacts, follow-through on those contacts and actual involvement in the school setting beyond the study' (Huberman 1994: 21). In addition to the communication skills required to produce materials for various non-specialist audiences, researcher competence draws on a variety of other interpersonal skills. These would include negotiation and interactive skills in terms of adopting an open attitude, being sensitive to the feelings and needs of others, allowing an equal opportunity for all to contribute, being able to accept criticism and working with self-confidence.

The significance of these competences in Huberman's model can be seen in the relationship between researcher and intermediaries. Intermediaries are individuals who are active in both research and professional settings and their role is to facilitate formal and informal contacts during the study. Intermediaries are necessary because they provide linkage mechanisms that enhance the potential usefulness of research findings. According to Huberman, this is particularly important early in a project in order that researchers are clear about how the study will converge with the concerns of the target audience. In addition, Huberman comments that it is important to recognize the on-going nature of sense-making and interpretative processes that are necessary to effective dissemination and take-up by ensuring that:

> During the study, it is these data that will form the meat of the exchanges, along with less-structured discussions about the research as a whole and its pertinence to local practice. During the analysis phase, a 'dissemination plan' is drawn up, with roles set out for each side, along with a discussion in depth of the findings most likely to challenge local norms and working arrangements. When the study is brought directly to the school settings, ideas are floated about what the study results can 'mean' in the local context, and what might be 'done' with them. During this time, members of the research team stay with the setting, typically to the point where both sides are going beyond the study.
>
> (Huberman 1994: 22)

Cousins and Simon (1996: 202) summarize the positive features that derive from improved linkages between practitioner and researchers in Huberman's sustained interactivity model as 'improved local practice, the generation of valid social science knowledge and intellectual stimulation, and conceptual development for researchers with concomitant implications for research programs and methodologies'. Nevertheless, they comment that these are theoretical benefits and empirical support remains relatively thin. With a particular focus on the impact of funding agency policies in the dissemination process, Cousins and Simon draw on their study of education and work in a changing society to understand how researcher-practitioner linkages can be encouraged and nurtured. In this respect, Cousins and Simon asked the following questions:

- How successful are policy inducements in fostering the development of researcher-practitioner partnerships? What is the nature of such partnerships? What factors influence partnership formation?
- What are the effects of policy-induced, researcher-practitioner partnerships on research practices and dissemination activities? Does partnership enhance the utility of research results?

(Cousins and Simon 1996: 202)

Overall, Cousins and Simon's findings suggest that despite support from both researchers and practitioners for a model of research that enhances collaboration and partnership, in practice 'the results show significant obstacles and contradictory dimensions inherent in policy-induced partnerships' (1996: 213). Cousins and Simon divide these obstacles into two areas. These are ideological and pragmatic barriers. The main ideological barriers were related to project control, intellectual ownership and the strategic intentions for data. These barriers were highly influential in determining the nature and impact of partnership arrangements. For example, Cousins and Simon note that the projects were primarily dominated by researchers and practitioner participation was primarily confined to data interpretation and dissemination. In this respect, Cousins and Simon reflect that 'researchers were very much invested in protecting their dominant role in the knowledge production function' (1996: 213). To a large extent, models of collaboration that relegate practitioners to consultancy roles were highly contributory to protecting researcher dominance. Cousins and Simon note that there are formidable pragmatic concerns that mitigate against the development of what they term true partnerships. These can be located in cultural differences whereby practitioner and researcher aims are at variance and in terms of the maintenance of on-going relationships that require 'not only sustained commitment from all partners but sufficient time for establishing and nurturing effective working relations' (Cousins and Simon 1996: 214).

Cousins and Simon's findings would support general critiques of the sustained interactivity model wherein there is a danger that the practitioner remains very much the client rather than the producer or initiator of research. Thus, whilst user needs are built into this model it retains the '. . . traditional boundaries of "research" and "user" communities' (Watkins 1994: 67). Moreover, this is a labour-intensive model that requires sustained but limited relationships to occur between researcher and researched. If research contracts allowed for the necessary time to be invested, and there are few signs that this is likely to be the case in most projects, such a model may bring benefits to those relatively few educational establishments and professionals involved. In this respect, Cousins and Simon note that an important finding of their study was that 'partnerships do conditionally affect the utilization of research data, and ultimately, dimensions of practice in ways that are both intended and helpful' (1996: 214).

However, there remains the issue of how the wider educational community would, or could, be involved and, in consequence, enhance dissemination. In order to confront these issues, Hargreaves (1999: 136) argues that 'If the objective is the creation of high-quality knowledge about effective teaching and learning that is applicable and actionable in classrooms, then practising teachers must be at the heart of this creation and researchers must get closer to them'. For Hargreaves (1999) therefore it is necessary to develop a model of dissemination that builds on what is termed *Mode 2* knowledge.

Evidence-based models of dissemination: Mode 2 knowledge model

I noted in Chapter 1 that there has been a significant move towards the valuing of what is called evidence-based research in education. This is the terrain that is of concern to Hargreaves (1999). Hargreaves comments that the dissemination of educational knowledge is currently in a poor state. This is because traditional dissemination models have become discredited due to their failure to facilitate the spread and take-up of knowledge of good practices. In this respect, Hargreaves highlights two features of dissemination that are crucial to effective dissemination. These are *transferability* and *transposability*. Transferability refers to the process whereby knowledge or practices move between people. Transposability refers to the process whereby knowledge or practices move between places. Hargreaves argues that successful dissemination requires both processes to be in operation at the same time. Thus, whilst it may not be uncommon for knowledge and practices to be successfully transferred between individuals in a particular organizational setting, greater difficulties occur when one seeks to transpose practices from one setting to another. This is because differences in context and situation may be substantial 'thus increasing the complexity of transposability; and the differences between the teaching staff of different schools (eg their values) increases the complexity of transferability' (Hargreaves 1999: 130).

Hargreaves uses the term 'tinkering' to demonstrate the processes of mobilization and conversion of tacit knowledge necessary for knowledge creation. By tinkering Hargreaves is referring to cycles of experimentation or the ad hoc testing out of alternative practices or possible solutions to a problem. Tinkering can be viewed at the individual level as central to the development of craft knowledge and expertise, but Hargreaves argues that 'When such tinkering becomes more systematic, more collective and *explicitly managed*, it is transformed into knowledge creation' (1999: 131, emphasis in original).

Hargreaves argues that more effective dissemination can be achieved by the development of what is called Mode 2 knowledge. Whereas Mode 1 knowledge is 'university-based, pure, disciplinary, homogenous, expert-led, supply-driven, hierarchical, peer-reviewed' (1999: 136), Mode 2 knowledge is 'applied, problem-focused, trans-disciplinary, heterogeneous, hybrid, demand-driven, entrepreneurial, accountability-tested, embedded in networks' (1999: 136). Thus:

> Mode 2 knowledge is not created and then applied; it evolves within the context of its application, but then may not fit neatly into Mode 1

knowledge structures. The team generating the knowledge may consist of people of very different backgrounds working together temporarily to solve a problem. The number of sites where such knowledge can be generated is greatly increased; they are linked by functioning networks of communication. The knowledge is then diffused most readily when the participants in its original production move to new situations and communicate through informal channels.

Hargreaves gives university researchers a key role in contributing to the development of this form of dissemination. Indeed, he comments that he cannot see how the networks and webs of professional knowledge creation that are so crucial to this model can be created unless universities take on the function for reconceptualizing 'both professional knowledge creation and its dissemination as the outcome of "tinkering networks" that need support and co-ordination' (Hargreaves 1999: 138).

The moves by both Huberman and Hargreaves to put the practitioner either into, or at the centre of, a knowledge production model replicate many of the concerns of both the reflective practitioner and action research literatures. For example, Schon's (1991) work on reflective practice has been concerned to 'accredit and make visible practitioners' experience, and challenges what he characterises as the dominant view of professional knowledge, based in positivist epistemology, which separates theory and research from the field of practice' (Issit 2002: 15). The concern with practice is also central to action research models where

> Action research may be used in almost any setting where a problem involving people, tasks and procedures cries out for solution, or where some change of feature results in a more desirable outcome. It can be undertaken by the individual teacher, a group of teachers working co-operatively within one school, or a teacher or teachers working alongside a researcher or researchers in a sustained relationship, possibly with other interested parties like advisers, university departments and sponsors on the periphery.
> (Cohen, Manion and Morrison 2000: 226)

However, whilst Huberman offers an interpretive approach that takes account of the practitioner, and Hargeaves seeks to reverse the traditional hierarchy of researcher-practitioner, neither Huberman nor Hargreaves challenge what Brown and Jones (2001: 169) call the 'singular dominant account'. This is a belief that research can tell us 'how it is' (Brown and Jones 2001: 169) so that we 'can then plan new strategies for the creation of new outcomes' (2001: 169). In this, neither Huberman nor Hargreaves challenge the imperialistic nature of what is perceived to be good or valid knowledge nor do they question the binaried nature of the power models they are using. With this in view, I turn to a discussion of the place of dissemination within models of research designed for social justice. I follow this with a discussion of how deconstructive approaches can usefully challenge predominant hierarchies of meaning associated with concepts of dissemination.

Dissemination and social justice

I have noted above the concern to include the practitioner in both Huberman's and Hargreaves' models of dissemination. For many working within educational research, this would not only be an important practice but it would be a key ethic of any research approach. For example, Griffiths (1998: 96) includes 'Openness to a wider community' in her list of principles for research designed to achieve social justice. Here she comments that 'Researchers need to be open to the viewpoints of all concerned with the research' (1998: 96). This not only includes the wider research community but also 'pupils, teachers, support staff, parents, LEA advisors, the neighbourhood, policy-makers and pressure groups' (1998: 96). Nevertheless, as Griffiths also clearly points out, such an approach needs to be combined with an awareness of the need to alter existing power relations in order to enhance social justice.

Research for social justice is commonly understood as encompassed within a critical research paradigm. Crotty (1998) suggests that we can understand this paradigm in two main ways. First, it offers a critique of the paradigms of positivism and interpretivism in terms that, whilst they seek to offer a way of knowing the social world, are not critical of the status quo. Secondly, critical inquiry is based on a conflict model of society that is concerned with social change. Crotty comments therefore that 'Critical inquiry [is not] a research that seeks merely to understand [it is] a research that challenges . . . that [takes up a view] of conflict and oppression . . . that seeks to bring about change' (1998: 112). Feminist, neo-Marxist, anti-racist and post-colonial approaches are included in the category of critical research.

An excellent example of approaches within the critical research paradigm is that of L. Smith (1999). Smith's work highlights the frustrations that indigenous peoples have experienced when dealing with various Western paradigms. In particular, her work is concerned with the political struggles that surround the legitimation of indigenous ways of knowing and being. Smith notes that an indigenous research agenda is concerned with four main issues. These are: survival, recovery, development and self-determination. These have arisen in response to, and as a critique of, the consequences of the assumed superiority of Western scientific models of knowledge. Thus:

> For Maori people, European conceptions of knowledge and of research have meant that, while being considered 'primitive', Maori

society has provided a fertile ground for research. The question of whose knowledge was being extended by research was of little consequence, as early ethnographers, educational researchers and occasional 'travellers' described, explained and recorded their accounts of various aspects of Maori society. Distortions of Maori social reality by ethnocentric researchers overly given to generalizations were initially apparent only to Maori people. While this type of research was validated by 'scientific method' and 'colonial affirmation', it did little to extend the knowledge of Maori people. Instead, it left a foundation of ideologically laden data about Maori society, which has distorted notions of what it means to be Maori.

(Smith 1999: 170)

Central to the ethical and political frameworks of post-colonial research approaches are issues of voice, authenticity and the ownership and shaping of knowledge systems that are appropriate to the cultural and historical mores of a community. Smith sets out a number of projects that are concerned with the development and validation of Maori approaches to creating knowledge and changing imperialistic power relations. These include the setting of research agendas by Maori people and the training of indigenous researchers. This has led to what are now called Kaupapa Maori approaches to research through which 'Maori people, as communities of the researched and as new communities of the researchers, have been able to engage in a dialogue about setting new directions for the priorities, policies, and practices of research, for, by and with Maori' (Smith 1999: 183; see also Bishop 1998).

Dissemination is an important activity to counter the exclusion experienced by marginalized groups from participating in the activities of the dominant non-indigenous society. For example, the Conventions on Biodiversity and GATT impact on indigenous communities but their concerns are not addressed in mainstream discussions nor are these communities necessarily aware of the existence of these issues. Here Smith notes two Kaupapa Maori research projects that are directly concerned with dissemination. These are 'Networking' and 'Sharing'. Networking is an important 'process which indigenous peoples have used effectively to build relationships and disseminate knowledge and information' (Smith 1999: 157). Networking builds knowledge and data bases but networks are also based on key Maori principles of relationships and connections. For example, Smith notes how networks are firstly initiated through face-to-face meetings as a way of not only checking an individual's political credentials but also their personality and spirit. 'Sharing' emphasizes knowledge as a collective benefit and as a form of resistance. Here, Smith notes that the face-to-face nature of sharing knowledge, through community gatherings such as weddings and funerals, remains vitally important to a marginalized community and this is supplemented with local newspapers and radio that is focused on indigenous issues. Overall, Smith notes that:

> Sharing is a responsibility of research. The technical term for this is the dissemination of results, usually very boring to non-researchers, very technical and very cold. For indigenous researchers sharing is about demystifying knowledge and information and speaking in plain terms to the community. Community gatherings provide a very daunting forum in which to speak about research. Oral presentations conform to cultural protocols and expectations. Often the audience may need to be involved emotionally with laughter, deep reflection, sadness, anger, challenges and debate. It is a very skilled speaker who can share openly at this level within the rules of the community.
>
> (Smith 1999: 161)

Deconstructing dissemination

My own primary research in the field of dissemination has very much drawn on collaborative work with colleagues in the health and social care sectors (see Barnes, Clouder, Hughes, Pritchard and Purkis 2003). Here we have been developing an understanding of the processes of dissemination in terms of a deconstructive model that can illuminate the ethical, political and communicative issues that lie at the heart of dissemination practices. Spivak (1999: 423) notes how deconstruction is a term coined by Jacques Derrida whose early writings 'examined how texts of philosophy, when they established definitions as starting points, did not attend to the fact that all such gestures involved setting each defined item off from all that it was not'. Thus, whilst a definition attempts to offer a fixed, and indeed closed, meaning, this meaning is actually drawn from an absent other. For example, the left hand column of Table 1 sets out some of the main meanings of dissemination that have already been explored in this chapter. However, the meanings in the left hand column draw on those listed on the right. The predominant meanings of dissemination that we have outlined above, therefore, invoke the trace or mark of those meanings in the right hand column.

In addition, this relational nature of meaning gives rise to an instability. Thus, 'the first term in a binary opposition can never be completely stable or secure, since it is dependent on that which is excluded' (Finlayson 1999: 64). As the main meanings of dissemination change, then, so do the meanings of what dissemination is not. For these reasons, deconstruction sees social life as a series of texts that can be read in a variety of ways and which, in consequence, give rise to a range of meanings. Moreover, each reading produces another text to the extent that we can view the social world as the

Table 1: The binaries of dissemination

Complete	Partial
Hard	Soft
End Point	Beginning
Formal	Informal
Authoritative	Powerless
Conclusive	Inconclusive
Public	Private
Structured	Unstructured
Rational	Irrational
Technical	Artful
Practical	Academic
Apolitical	Political
Universal	Contextual

Source: Barnes, Clouder, Hughes, Pritchard and Purkis, 2003

emanations of a whole array of intertextual weavings. This is an important point in terms of how we might think about political challenges to meaning as it draws attention to the potential of change rather than stasis.

However, whilst there is a variety of meanings, binaries are organized in terms of a hierarchy. As I have indicated, the meanings in the left hand column are ascendant. It is important here to note that deconstruction does not seek to overturn the binary through a reversal of dominance. This would simply maintain hierarchization. Deconstruction is concerned to illustrate how language is used to frame meaning. Politically, its purpose is to lead to 'an appreciation of hierarchy as illusion sustained by power. It may be a necessary illusion, at our stage in history. We do not know. But there is no rational warrant for assuming that other imaginary structures would not be possible' (Boyne 1990: 124).

To achieve this, deconstruction involves three phases (Grosz 1990). The first two of these are the reversal and displacement of the hierarchy. In terms of reversal we might, for example, seek to reclaim the terms on the right of Table 1 for more positive interpretations of their meanings in relation to dissemination. However it is insufficient simply to try to reverse the hier-archical status of any binary. At best, this simply keeps hierarchical organ-ization in place. At worst, such attempts will be ignored because the domin-ant meanings of a hierarchical pairing are so strongly in place. This is why it is necessary to displace common hierarchized meanings. This is achieved by displacing the 'negative term, moving it from its oppositional role into the very heart of the dominant term' (Grosz 1990: 97). The purpose of this is to make clear how the subordinated term is subordinated. This requires a third phase. This is the creation of a new term.

A primary purpose of our collaborative work has been to use the dualistic framing of dissemination to illustrate that the subordinate side of the binary is worthy of exploration. In this, our work has been focused on the second stage of deconstruction that Grosz (op. cit.) has set out. Thus, we have been working at reversing and displacing, but not replacing, predominant meanings. To achieve this we have been concerned to illustrate how the everyday processes of qualitative research can be reconfigured as dissemination.

Here our work has demonstrated how issues of dissemination are embedded in all stages of qualitative research. To illustrate this we gave a series of examples drawn from our own research experiences, two of which I shall outline here.

We began our deconstructive exercise by reversing the notion that dissemination occurs at the end of a qualitative research project by outlining how dissemination also occurs at the beginning of research. This is because the kinds of literature and ideas that we draw on when designing research are also aspects of a dissemination chain. In this respect, we noted how the incorporation of ideas of social justice and empowerment at the design stage of a research project undertaken by one of us was the consequence of dissemination. Understanding dissemination as a beginning point allows us to pay attention to how, and which, ideas are disseminated when undertaking literature reviews and how they are subsequently incorporated, modified or adapted in the design and execution of research.

In terms of reversing the idea that dissemination should be conceived as a conclusive, formal and highly controlled phase of research, we argued that dissemination might be more appropriately acknowledged as somewhat less conclusive, informal and rather more difficult to control than we might want to believe. The example we gave focused on data that demonstrated how a research respondent acted upon comments made by one of us during an interview. Such a situation is traditionally considered to be a problematic, but inevitable, aspect of qualitative research through which the researcher exercises influence in the field. The common solution to this is to write a reflexive account of the researcher's role. However, we sought to rename 'researcher influence' as 'dissemination'. In particular, we noted that the concern with the development of reflexivity amongst researchers has directed our attention away from considering the researched as reflexive individuals who will contemplate ideas disseminated in interviews and may even change their practices accordingly. Within such a view, dissemination can be viewed as a reflexive and on-going conversation that one has with others as much as oneself.

Overall, the purpose of our paper was to raise a critique of dissemination models that are based on technical rationalist ontologies. This was because we believe they privilege a particularly narrow set of meanings and, in consequence, preclude other ways through which we might imagine dissemination acts. In so doing, our purpose was not to replace the predominant meanings of dissemination as a relatively complete, apolitical, formal act or process that occurs primarily at the end-point of research and through which the researcher is viewed as an authoritative bearer of knowledge. To do so would maintain an oppositional, albeit reversed, hierarchy of meaning as set out in Table 1. Rather, our purpose has been to add to these by bringing into the centre those more subordinated and negative meanings that are commonly assumed to be what dissemination is not. Overall, our aim was to raise the thought that dissemination is present at the very moment of conceptualizing research and continues in ways we have yet to explore well after the formal stages of research are complete.

Conclusion

I began this chapter by raising a question. Should we understand the naming of a day nursery near to where I live as an aspect of dissemination or diffusion? Certainly, there are those who would wish to keep a strong distinction between the meaning of these terms and to emphasize how dissemination is, or at least should be, a systematic and regulated process. Yet, the development of the models I have outlined indicates, perhaps overwhelmingly, the complexities inherent in the take-up, or otherwise, of ideas and practices. Paradoxically, of course, the very desire to produce a model suggests how powerfully we believe in the possibilities of, at least imperfect, control.

I have also sought to highlight how we cannot dismiss what we understand to be the nature of knowledge, and how this is produced, from an understanding of dissemination. The models discussed in this chapter rest on particular notions of how we might conceptualize knowledge and, in consequence, what are appropriate methodologies for understanding the social world. Moreover, although predominantly an understanding of dissemination is premised on a rather apolitical, benign view of knowledge transfer and, contemporarily, there is much concern with including the practitioner in the dissemination cycle, dissemination cannot be divorced from issues of power and ethics. This view of dissemination, my view if you like, suggests that dissemination is not simply an end or beginning point but is central to the processes of knowledge production.

PART II

3 | Dissemination and identity – tales from the school gates

Carrie Paechter

Introduction

I come to this chapter from two directions, each being related to aspects of my own identity. The first is a professional concern that there is an important audience for my own and others' work that is very difficult to reach. As a feminist researcher working in the field of gender and education, I am increasingly of the view that parents, and particularly mothers, are a vital factor in producing the sorts of change, in society at large and the education system in particular, that would lead to more equitable lives for future generations. Although of course they are not the only influences on their children's behaviour, gendered or otherwise (Harris 1998), parents are still important shapers of the context in which a child spends her or his early years. Mothers, in particular, are important influences on schools, as they interact with children's teachers to work to support their children and solve problems inside and outside of school (Dudley-Marling 2001; Reay 1998). So if mothers can be convinced that the gender regimes prevailing in school are both pernicious and amenable to change, they are key participants in this change process. Thus as a feminist researcher with a particular interest in gender and schooling, I see mothers as an important group to whom I wish to communicate my ideas.

At the same time, there are times in my daily life when I am positioned as a mother among mothers. In these situations I often find that in order to fit in I have to sideline aspects of my self, in particular those aspects of my professional self that are particularly concerned with disseminating ideas about gender and schooling. This means that in situations where I have the most straightforward access to this key audience, I am actually unable to communicate with them about the topics I would like to discuss. In this paper I want to explore some of the contradictions between these two positions and the conflicts involved in addressing them, separately and together.

I should point out at this stage that it is my voice that I am foregrounding in this paper, and it could be argued that in doing so I privilege the already privileged. There is also a possibility (related, I think, to the discourses about motherhood that I will discuss later) that my approach to this issue will appear patronizing. I hope you will bear with my argument and come to agree with me that it is not. It is precisely because of the ways in which discourses about mothers are currently constructed that any challenge to mothers' individual beliefs can be seen as patronizing; this is part of the issue that I want to address here. Nevertheless, it is likely that the other participants in school-gate social life would view the situation differently, and we need to be aware of this. We also need to be aware that there is another group of mothers absent from this story: those who work hours that do not permit them to drop off their children or pick them up from school. They will have different investments, and may have a completely different story to tell.

In order to tease out some of the issues involved in these contradictions, I want first to set out the two positions in which I find myself, and the discourses through which they are constructed. I will then go on to consider how these roles conflict in the specific situations of informal, child-focused contacts with other mothers, such as at the school gates, in parenting support groups and on social occasions.

It is widely established (Acker 1994; Dudley-Marling 2001; Lewis 1991; Marshall 1991; Miller 1997; Raddon 2001b) that there are conflicts between motherhood and professional roles. Discussion, however, has tended to focus on organizational issues (such as promotion and childcare), on the effects on the mother of such things as guilt, the 'double shift' and the dilution of identity, particularly career-related identities, and on potential changes in employed mothers' relationships with their children. In all cases, the worlds of the home and the workplace are perceived essentially as separate, although one may 'invade' the other to a lesser or greater extent (Massey 2001) (through a parent taking work home or taking time off to care for a sick child). While it is recognized in these discussions that the world of the home is not expected to impinge (or at least no more than can be helped) on the world of the workplace, there is no concomitant recognition that there can be pressure to maintain the exclusion of professional matters from the social worlds of and around the home. It is on this latter issue, and its implications for the effective dissemination of my research, that I wish to focus in this chapter.

On 'being an academic'

My sense of personal and professional self is related to a series of shorthand descriptions which I use for self-labelling. 'Being an academic' is one, as are 'being a feminist' and 'having knowledge about gender and about gender and education'. These descriptions are central not only to my professional identity but also to my identity more generally, as a woman with a career, as a woman with children, and so on. Raddon (2001b) notes that while academics who are also mothers may feel guilt at continuing to be focused on and enjoy academic life, at the same time they may feel that it is at work rather than at home that they feel fundamentally themselves; their (our) identity is bound up very closely with the academy. So my academic identity follows me into the playground with my children; it cannot simply be abandoned when I am primarily operating as a mother. I am thus not moving between subject positions but inhabiting several simultaneously, of which (at least) the two on which I am focusing here are partly contradictory (Acker 1994). These various subjectivities are themselves positioned within and constitutive of a number of discourses. Of particular salience here are the implications of having an academic identity, the relationship between the academic and the rest of the world, and discourses about the importance and relevance of academic work in gender and education. I will contrast these later in the chapter with the competing discourses of the 'good mother'.

'Being an academic' as a description of aspects of my identity brings with it a number of assumptions and values about what is important in academic life and what it means to claim these for myself. Acker (1994) characterizes the academy as being (as is the family) a 'greedy institution', one that demands total commitment. This commitment is measured, particularly in the early and middle stages of an academic career, in terms of research output (Acker 1994; Raddon 2001b). So being an academic is fundamentally bound up with carrying out high-level, original, academic research. While it is acknowledged that the academy is constructed as a masculinist institution with conventions and practices that marginalize women, particularly those with families (Acker 1994; Brooks 1997a; Heward 1994; Heward et al. 1997), nonetheless as an academic with a permanent post, my current (though not my previous (Reay 2000)) experience of this marginalization is partial. I feel secure in my academic identity, and though it is clear that I am working in fields (gender and education) that are themselves marginal in the academy, I continue to feel fully part of the institution. Consequently I do claim and identify with an academic identity and value much of what this implies, for example my ability to speak, read and write in specialist registers, use particular vocabularies, understand and discuss the key issues in my field. Saying that one is an academic implies that one lives, at least part of the time, in a world apart, a world to which most members of the public do not have access. It implies expertise, specialist knowledge – and I experience pleasure as a result of my 'mastery' of this.

I am aware, however, that the specialist registers that we use are exclusionary, and that many people (some of my students, for example) are unhappy about having to learn this esoteric way of speaking and writing in order to take part in academic debate. While I enjoy my own ability to work within these registers, which enable discussions to take place that I value and which excite me academically (Griffiths 1992), I would also like everyone to have my specialist knowledge. It is significant to me, and I would like to imagine that it would be so to others, if only they had access to it. So getting this sort of specialist knowledge across to non-academics has personal importance to me. My academic self includes simultaneously a fascination with ideas, with the abstract, and a desire to bring these abstractions to bear on concrete issues and problems that people, including myself, come up against in their everyday lives.

The need to feel socially and personally worthwhile is a key aspect of identity (Johnson 1995). People need to believe that what they do is important, and I am no exception to this; I want to feel that what I work so hard at actually matters in and to the world, including to the world outside of academia. Furthermore, work within applied fields such as education gets much of its *raison d'être* from the very possibility of application; there seems little point in doing it if it does not get beyond the university. Thus, part of the way in which I understand the self-description of 'academic carrying out research about gender and schooling' includes some sense that the findings of the research should reach those for whom it might be useful or important. In my view, this includes parents. Parents need to know what goes on in schools, how their children are disciplined by gender regimes within them, how young people can be undermined and even damaged by prevailing heterosexist discourses around particular stereotypes of masculinity and femininity, how so much of how we choose to bring our children up is mediated by the practices of the classroom and the playground (Delamont 1990; Paechter 1998). This specialist knowledge about how gender regimes operate within schools is something which I feel I have a duty (as a feminist) to pass on, because it will help others to challenge the gendered discourses through which schools operate. It also affects my own parenting; I believe acting on what I know can help bring about a more equitable society for future generations. Clearly this is more likely to happen if I can get others to change their parenting practices in similar ways. I therefore have both a personal and a professional interest in disseminating my work on gender and education to other parents.

On 'being a mother'

Discourses around motherhood are very different to those focused around academia and the academic career (Raddon 2001b). Here, worthwhileness is construed in relation to the child, with a particular focus on the mother-child bond. In these discourses, attention is drawn to the importance of the mother in the child's life and to her unique responsiveness to the child's needs. Lewis (1991) notes that the ideal mother is constructed as not working outside the home, and that even when it is acknowledged that some mothers do undertake paid work, ideologies of motherhood treat it as always being of secondary importance. Within the 'greedy institution' (Acker 1994) of the family, the position of the 'good mother' is as an individual whose interests are identical with those of her baby (Marshall 1991) and whose identity is therefore intimately intermeshed with those of her children; having a significant professional identity does not enter the picture at all. Through discourses of motherhood, women are positioned as responsible not only for the care of their children but also for their future development (Burman 1994) and success in school (Dudley-Marling 2001). In this sense motherhood is perceived as an all-important career in itself. Miller (1997) notes that

> Becoming an NCT[1] mother commonly involves months of preparation, including attendance at classes, reading relevant magazines or books and listening to many comparative stories about other people's experience of giving birth . . . This may assist in the . . . birth of a new form of adult – the mother.
>
> (Miller 1997: 69)

This level of preparation resembles (though in truncated form) professional training. In the popular childcare literature, although the idea that mothers may go out to work is now treated as an acceptable option (some women writers, for example (Einon 1988) even admit that they themselves worked while their children were small), having a career outside the home may still be treated as only undertaken out of financial necessity and remains widely perceived as being in conflict with the mother role (Lewis 1991; Marshall 1991). It is uncommon, for example, for women with young children to admit to enjoying their work or to being ambitious; the discourse is one of financial necessity rather than personal fulfilment. This positions as 'bad mothers' those of us for whom paid work is at least as important for personal fulfilment as it is for family finances. If we admit this we are in danger of becoming marginalized as mothers, outside of the acceptable parameters of motherhood ideologies. Burman (1992) notes in this regard that women's assertion of power or independence is seen as damaging children's self-confidence; in the discourses of motherhood, where the child always comes first, a mother's independent existence becomes very problematic.

Because of the stress on the unique responsiveness of the mother to her children's needs, coupled with the disjunction between the lack of status of mothers within society and the importance of the mother role in discourses of childrearing, parental, and specifically maternal, knowledge is accorded enormous status in childcare texts. While a relatively recent phenomenon and in part a reaction to earlier, more didactic attitudes to parents (Hardyment 1995), it is now a major feature of the discourse. This privileged knowledge is both seen as arising out of the parent-child bond and juxtaposed with the more general, theoretical knowledge of experts:

As you watch and listen to her, think about and adjust yourselves to her, you are laying the foundations of a new member of your own race and of a friendship that can last forever. You are going to know this person better than you will ever know anybody else.

(Leach 1997: 10)

You should judge for yourself what is best, always remembering that what is needed for the child next door may be totally different to what is appropriate for your own child.

(Green 1988: 175)

Nobody knows your child like you do. Only parents know how their children behave day by day, know their characters, their likes and dislikes, their difficulties and achievements. Doctors, health visitors and other professionals caring for children don't have that kind of knowledge.

(Health Education Authority 1994: 29)

This discourse around parenthood has a number of practical implications for relations between parents and between experts and parents, even where experts are explicitly present in that role. The first is that where parents' perceptions conflict with those of experts, expert knowledge is dismissed as irrelevant, either in general, or to these parents' situation. For example, many parents believe that they treated their sons and daughters identically from birth, and that any gender differences were not only apparent from the outset but also an inherent part of the child's makeup. My own attempts to bring research findings suggesting the opposite into social discussions around this have been either rebuffed or treated with the sort of amusement reserved for those who never leave their ivory towers for the real world. Dissonance of this kind is thereby resolved in favour of parental perceptions; the most acknowledgement one gets is a grudging suggestion that 'this may be what the research suggests in general, but I know that I treated my children the same from the start, and they have still turned out different'. In many ways this is not surprising. Middle-class parents in particular claim at least to want their daughters to be strong and independent and their sons to grow up gentle; it is hard to live with the idea that, despite one's efforts, they are being educated in aspects of stereotypical femininity and masculinity (Miller 1997).

Secondly, even officially framed discussions between experts and parents about the care of particular children take place in an atmosphere in which criticism of someone else's parenting is taboo. This means that the expert may have to put some of her or his expertise to one side in discussions with parents. The priority given to parental knowledge means that it is sometimes not possible to recommend the best thing for the child, but only the best thing within the parameters in which the parent is operating. This taboo operates not only in the field of child behaviour but also in areas that are of necessity expert-led, such as nutrition. During an observation of health visitor[2] training in a clinic, for example, I heard the trainer (a senior health visitor) suggest to her trainee that it would be counterproductive to advise a parent not to give her baby fruit juice (despite the expert view that it is unnecessary and bad for teeth); as the parent had already decided to give the juice, the best approach would be to advise that the mother make it extremely dilute. A suggestion that the baby would be better off drinking water, would, it was implied, not be heard.

A third implication, which relates to this, is the assumption that if expert advice conflicts with parental beliefs or choices, the conflict arises from the lack of practical experience of the experts. Health visitors seem particularly to suffer from this belief that either they are childless themselves and have no experience of the realities of childcare, or that they fail to practice what they preach.[3] The distrust of female experts in particular may also be associated with the dissonances between discourses of women as experts with careers and discourses around the sensitive mother responding to her child. For those working in the childcare professions, such as health visitors, the conflicts between discourses of the 'good mother' and the 'professional woman' are particularly pressing, and have a direct affect on the conduct of their professional lives. Health visitors who have young children (as many do, it being a common career move for midwives who find that profession, with its shifts and sometimes unpredictable hours of work, incompatible with family responsibilities) operate within and in support of discourses of the 'good mother' but at the same time are themselves constructed, as working women, as 'bad mothers'. This undermines the perceived value of the advice they give, even when their professional advice is filtered through their own parental experience. The discourse of the 'good mother', ever-present in the baby clinic, asks them directly: how could someone who has spent time acquiring such expertise possibly also have been able to forge a strong bond with her own children – and if she has not, what right does she have to advise us?

Outside of 'official' advice-giving and support arenas, in discussions about childcare between parents, discourses of 'common sense' and privileged parental knowledge of their own children reign to an even greater extent. Parents may know about or read expert views about child development, infant nutrition and so forth, but these are sifted against both received wisdom and personal experience. Where there is conflict, the expert view is generally rejected. This makes parents a particularly difficult group to reach with ideas that are in conflict with prevailing prejudices.

Conflict, roles and identities in the playground

So how do these discourses come together in terms of my conflicting identities as both mother and expert in informal encounters with other mothers? In examining this I am going to start by telling two stories:

Story one: Choosing a primary school

I live in the overlap between the catchment areas of two primary schools. My stepdaughters went to one of these, and it was assumed for a long time, by myself and my partner, by the school, and by other parents, that my sons would do the same. In the event, however, we decided we preferred the alternative school, and sent our elder son there. At the time of this decision I regularly took my stepdaughters to school, and was friendly with other mothers in the playground. They knew that I had expert knowledge about schools and my choice against this school (about which some of them also had growing doubts) was greeted with a good deal of interest. Over the next few months I was asked by several parents about the reasons for our decision. Their interest, however, seemed to be sustained only as long as I could give 'gut'-type explanations (we didn't like the new head) which they might themselves have experienced. Those reasons, in many ways more important for me, concerned with the organization of the school, the ways in which reading was taught, the school's attitude to the literacy hour, their approach to mathematics, seemed to be of lesser interest to other parents, and I often found that people started to switch off if I raised these.

Story two: Everyone's reading Steve Biddulph

When Steve Biddulph's book *Raising Boys* (Biddulph 1997) first came out in this country, it raised a good deal of interest among parents. Copies were passed around my friends, some of whom took a lot of his ideas on board. I read it myself, and it made me profoundly uncomfortable. Biddulph comes from a completely different school of thought to myself as regards gender, and is particularly keen to stress the effects of testosterone, thus in my view naturalizing and indeed in some senses valorizing some of the more problematic aspects of male behaviour:

> Testosterone equals vitality, and it's our job to honour it and steer it into healthy directions
>
> (Biddulph 1997: 47)

His view of adult gender roles is also traditional in some respects. Fathers, while seen as fully participating in childrearing, are expected to be conventionally (and hegemonically) masculine role models for their sons. Good fathers are presented as acting to support mothers who find it difficult to deal with testosterone-filled teenage boys and as carrying out stereotypically masculine activities with their sons:

> If you don't know things like fishing or making stuff in sheds or fixing go-carts or computers and so on, well, you can learn together.
>
> (Biddulph 1997: 67)

Consequently, I viewed the ascendence of this book, just at the time of greatest moral panic about male underachievement, with alarm. This alarm affected both aspects of my identity: as a feminist educationalist and as a mother. As a feminist educationalist I felt that if these ideas gained ascendency among parents they would influence how they brought up their sons, which in turn would make for even more restrictive student-policed gender regimes within schools (Lloyd and Duveen 1992; Walker 1988). As a mother I felt that I did not want my sons to grow up in a community in which male aggression was tolerated as something that was 'natural' and inevitable, something which had to be 'honoured' and channelled rather than challenged.

As an expert, I have enormous academic resources to challenge Biddulph's book. While not having his mass audience, I am quite able to marshall arguments and evidence against his assertions; I could write a counter-text with relative ease. As a mother talking to friends, however, I did not find it easy to challenge his influence. Parents who take on Biddulph's ideas (or those of any other parenting guru) have decided to bring up their children in a particular way. To challenge Biddulph is therefore to challenge their parenting practice, to break a taboo. I therefore was and remain all but silenced.

The school playground in the morning is for me where the discourses of mother and expert meet on a daily basis. Although other people (fathers, grandparents, childminders) are involved in taking children to school, this is predominantly a world of mothers. At the school gates we are identified almost entirely as mothers, our 'other selves' relegated or even absent:

> At school the other day Danielle's mum, who I often talk with in the playground, asked me if it was I who had waved to her in town earlier in the week. She said, 'I thought to myself, I think that's Robyn's mum, but you'd gone before I could wave back'. A trivial enough incident perhaps but here are two women, both in their late 30s, one a senior

nurse, the other a lecturer, who don't know each other's names and who identify each other in terms of their respective children. Being defined and identified in terms of someone else means not being seen as a person in your own right, with your own desires, hopes, aspirations, abilities, achievements, shortcomings, aptitudes, sadnesses and so on.

(Sikes 1997: 37)

For me in particular, it is my expert self that is absent from the mother/child-focused world of the before-school playground. Because most women in full-time employment do not have the opportunity to take their children to school on a regular basis, the mothers whom I meet in this particular context are, with few exceptions, either full-time mums or have jobs that are significantly part-time. Those who work outside the home either work hours short enough to fit into the length of a school day, or at night, once their partners are available to take over the childcare. For these women, motherhood is (at least at present) their primary career. They have usually been at home at least since their second child was born, and thus have significant investments in the discourses of motherhood and the primacy of the mother-child relationship. While some were never career-focused and might have been very glad to leave work when their children were born, all have made sacrifices in terms of personal freedom, work companionship and financial independence in order to care for their children. In many ways, motherhood is at present their primary career; their investment in it parallels my own investment in my academic work (Miller 1997). Furthermore, because they work predominantly in the home, these women are more likely to have traditionally gendered domestic arrangements, with male partners at work full-time. As a result they are also more likely to have at least some (though possibly ambivalent) commitment to the gender order that my research seeks to challenge.

Although these women are in many respects very different to me, I want to fit in with them. I like them. My son plays with their children. I want to have a part in the mutual support network that flourishes as a result of these informal school-gate relationships. Despite our differences, I would like to be accepted as one of them. However, in order to do this I have to 'pass', to appear to share their beliefs at least some of the time. This means at least overtly subscribing to or at least not directly challenging some of the received wisdom about childrearing; in particular, it means sidelining much of what I know about children, about gender and about schooling.

Having to 'pass' means *at the least* playing down aspects of oneself. By 'playing down', I mean acting as if aspects of oneself do not exist, or are utterly irrelevant.

(Griffiths 1995: 117)

This playing down of my expert self is particularly problematic because this group of women is representative of a wider audience that I particularly want my research to reach. They are heavily involved in their children's upbringing, so if I can persuade them to accept my ideas about gender relations and how they affect our parenting (rather than, for example, Steve Biddulph's), then maybe some parenting practices might change – with the eventual possibility of a more equitable society. They are also important influences on schools, through their presence as classroom helpers, their constancy at the gates, their vociferousness when things go wrong, their commitment to the PTA and their presence on governing bodies (Dudley-Marling 2001). If they can be convinced that there are ways of changing prevailing gender regimes in schools, and that it is important to do so, again, we might be able to bring about long-term change. Finally, even though I have yet to find a way of reaching them with my ideas, other people have done so, and their influence needs to be challenged.

Bringing expert knowledge about things that matter to parents, into parent-focused arenas, poses difficult challenges. I need to find a way of being with other mothers that permits me to be one of them while retaining my expert voice, allowing it to contribute to the discussion. This is of course a common problem for those concerned to disseminate educational (and other) research. Griffiths suggests that researchers working with teachers will need to 'learn to talk in different registers when we need to' (Griffiths 1992: 33). The problem for me, however, is that registers are not just about vocabulary, but reflect important and powerful discourses. They bring with them assumptions about what is appropriate to say and how it is appropriate to say it, who can speak and who cannot. And until I can find a way of bringing my expert voice into the register of school-gate parentspeak, I will remain unable to disseminate my work to what in many ways is my most important audience.

Notes

1 The National Childbirth Trust is a campaigning organization with a focus on better childbirth and perinatal care for mothers and babies. It offers classes in childbirth, breastfeeding support and advice, and local support groups for young parents. The 'NCT mother' is a stereotype with some basis in fact. Such a mother will typically try to avoid interventions in the birthing process, breastfeed her baby and place high importance on things such as healthy eating and educational play. I am an NCT mother myself and, apart from going back to work full-time soon after the birth of my first child, fit the stereotype fairly closely.

2 Health checks and clinic visits are an important feature of early parenthood in the UK. They serve the dual role of checking that babies are developing as expected, and supporting parents, especially mothers. Health visitors, who run these clinics, also have an educational and advice-giving role, for which they have specialized, degree-level training, including the study of child health and development, on top of an initial qualification in nursing.

3 There may be some limited grounds for this belief. I was once told by a health visitor that the 'controlled crying technique' (Green 1992), which she was strongly advocating as a means for getting babies and young children to sleep through the night, was not something she could have borne to carry out with her own children.

4 | The creation and dissemination of feminist research in education: facts or fictions?

Becky Francis

Introduction

Issues around the purpose and nature of feminist research dissemination are explored in this chapter. 'Feminism' means different things to different people, and various types of feminist have different goals, as well as differing preferences of method by which to achieve those goals. It is unsurprising, then, that there is no single agreed form of feminist research methodology. Rather, feminist researchers adopt different research approaches depending on their theoretical perspective (Stanley and Wise 1993). Yet despite this diversity, there is agreement that some key concerns feature in all feminist research. One of these is the emancipatory intention of feminist research (Maynard and Purvis 1994; Francis 1999). The feminist movement itself has emancipatory aims, in that it seeks to identify and challenge gender discrimination and inequity (Assiter 1996). Feminist research is a method by which to pursue those aims, making feminist research itself an emancipatory endeavour. So in disseminating their research findings, feminist researchers usually hope to challenge or to change the status quo. And in terms of the practice of this act of dissemination, feminists often stress the importance of the application of high ethical standards both during data collection and dissemination of feminist research findings (Maynard 1994; Lynch 1999).

Yet some of these perceptions of research and the purposes of dissemination can be questioned by postmodern theories. This chapter seeks to explore the implications of the application of such theories. It begins by discussing the generally accepted feminist stance on research dissemination, and then goes on to explain the ways in which some of these assumptions have been problematized by poststructuralist thinking. In analysing the implications of these theoretical applications, I shall argue that both humanist and poststructuralist perspectives on research are limited, and will suggest some alternative ways of conceiving research outputs and dissemination.

Dissemination of feminist research

One of the manifestations of the feminist emphasis on ethical practice in research dissemination is the practice of 'taking research back'. Many feminists believe that the communication of their research findings to their respondents is an essential aspect of their research dissemination (Lynch 1999). 'Taking research back', as this process is often termed, is seen as positive for a number of reasons. First, it means that the respondents have the opportunity to reflect upon and learn from the research findings, with the chance that they will find the new knowledge empowering. Secondly, it is a reciprocal act, limiting the extent to which respondents are simply used by the researcher and then dispensed with.

Even at a surface level, such processes are not always so unproblematic as is sometimes supposed. As we have seen, feminist research is unashamedly political and emancipatory in its intentions. However, as Assiter (1996) has observed, emancipation is a relative concept: what is experienced as emancipatory for one group might be experienced as oppressive by another. It is likely, then, that some of our respondents will not approve of the perspective we take to our findings, or the use that we make of those findings in furthering our feminist intentions. Feedback to respondents may also be tokenistic or impeded for a variety of reasons, and there is rarely full discussion of these processes in research reports.

These problems may be compounded in educational research (such as my own), where research is often conducted in a school setting, and respondents are often children and young people. Although feminist researchers concerned with ethical practice may ask the pupils themselves whether they wish to participate in the research, giving pupils the option to abstain (rather than, say, a teacher simply picking pupil respondents), pupils are far more likely to agree to participate than they would be in other environments. Given the choice between lessons and an interview, it is hardly surprising that many students opt for the latter. There is, then, an element of coercion involved. This is even more the case on occasions when students may not have the option whether or not to participate in research. For example, my last research project involved the observation of classroom behaviour (Francis 2000). Pupils had no option but to attend the lessons, and therefore could not avoid participating in the research. This criticism could be applied to much ethnographic research in schools.

Other practical issues relating to dissemination have sometimes undermined my ethical intentions during research in schools. For example, when attempting to 'take research back', I have found that many schools have not time even to arrange for the researcher to present findings to teachers, let alone to facilitate feedback to the respondents (children) concerned. A further example relating to dissemination is the way in which pupils sometimes question the notion of respondent anonymity. While an ethical approach usually includes the guarantee of anonymity to respondents, I have found that school pupils often articulate a desire to be named in publications, and are excited at that prospect. This raises complex considerations: on the one hand, it could be argued that pupils do not understand how their responses might reflect badly on them. However, to override their wishes is to exercise a power relationship, and to deny pupils what is, from their point of view, a potentially beneficial outcome of the research dissemination.

Hence even the application of a relatively simplistic reading of the purpose and methods of feminist research dissemination can raise many practical problems. However, these are arguably minor in comparison with some of the theoretical challenges brought to bear on many feminist readings of dissemination by recent trends in philosophical thought.

The impact of postmodernist theory on feminist research

The traditional, positivist representation of social research has been one where the researcher enters 'the field' as an 'objective' observer. The researcher gathers data from respondents or secondary sources, analyses this data in order to discover trends or to identify answers to research questions, and then disseminates the findings in order to contribute to the body of learned knowledge in this area. It is assumed that a 'true' picture, and clear facts, can be uncovered and articulated by research. Feminist researchers have made scathing and influential criticisms of this view. They have demonstrated the androcentric nature of much social research, which produces knowledge that is presented as objective fact, but which on closer interrogation can be revealed as reflecting masculinist assumptions and values (Eichler 1988; Harding 1991; Stanley and Wise 1993).

However, some feminist research has in its turn has been criticized for presenting particular views (which marginalize certain groups) as 'truths'. Working class, ethnic minority, lesbian and disabled feminists have maintained that much feminist research dissemination reflects a white, middle-class, heterosexual and able-bodied perspective at the expense of 'others' (see, for example, Hooks 1982; Walkerdine and Lucey 1989; Mirza 1997). The presentation of a coherent feminist founding subject, 'womanhood', has been revealed to be a fallacy which masks differences and power inequalities between women. Such criticism has been compounded by the impact of postmodern theories. These perspectives have provided the theoretical tools with which to deconstruct such 'total' modernist positions. Moreover, when taken to their full (relativist) conclusions, postmodernist perspectives question the very point of social research. They ask whether there is any 'real' world on which we as researchers seek to comment, and whether there are universal values or truths which can ever be assumed, discovered or pursued. As I noted above, feminist research has an emancipatory purpose, in that it seeks to disseminate new knowledge about gender relations in order to provoke change. Some postmodern theories challenge these assumptions. In my work elsewhere I have explored and debated the theoretical challenges brought by one theory that falls under the 'postmodern' umbrella: poststructuralism (Francis 1999; 2001a; 2001b; 2002). The key points of tension are as follows.

Feminism's emancipatory narrative can be seen as an example of what Foucault has termed modernist 'grand narratives'. It is a narrative which presents a coherent view of the world, and makes claims to a 'true' and moral account (for example, about the universality and injustice of gender discrimination). Although feminism has revealed the way in which many of the humanist, enlightenment values that dominate Western society reflect masculine versions of knowledge and truth, feminism also draws on humanist values of justice and human rights in order to argue for gender equity (see Balbus 1989; Soper 1990; Assiter 1996; Hey 1999; Raphael-Reed 2001). Ideologies, even 'liberational' ones, and the social movements upon which they are based, are problematized as naïve and even oppressive modernist grand narratives by poststructuralist theory. Poststructuralist theory is 'relativist', in that it sees such narratives as socially constructed discourses or stories rather than as valid 'truths'. To many poststructuralists, truth discourses or 'grand narratives' exercise a coercive power relationship (as they make totalitarian claims to moral 'right' or truth), and consequently require deconstruction.

Poststructuralist theory also questions the assumption of human agency evoked in the notion of emancipatory endeavour. Jones (1997) and Hood-Williams (1998) observe that such notions of agency are based on the humanist (modernist) concept of a self which is an already existing individual. In contrast, poststructuralists reject the notion of individual, meaning-making personalities. Rather, they see the self as simply constructed in relations of power through discourses: we do not actively choose which discourses we take up and use. The belief that we have our own coherent, meaning-making personalities is simply due to our positioning within discourses of liberal, humanist individualism (Jones 1997).

The challenge of poststructuralist theory can be applied beyond research with emancipatory intentions, and to research per se. If all truth is relative, and there is no 'real' world which we research (only objects constituted by discourse, see Parker 1992), then all researchers are doing are producing stories about the world. Our 'dissemination of findings' is not the articulation of an authentic reality, but the construction of an account of society which cannot be seen as having any more or less validity than other accounts. Hence research dissemination is actually story-telling. (Indeed, I have on many occasions heard postmodernist researchers referring to their research as 'stories' when presenting their work at conferences.) In applying a relativist position on value, no one story can be seen as having more merit or value than another: all are simply discursive products, produced according to the subject's (researcher's) position in discourse.

If one accepts this argument, one could question whether we require respondents in our research at all. If, rejecting notions of validity and 'the real', social research is simply the creation of stories, it could be pursued without recourse to respondents (or even to 'the field'). Indeed, it could be argued that respondents are being misled when invited to participate or cooperate with postmodernist research: they participate in the belief that they are contributing to a quest for knowledge and 'truth', rather than as accessories to a story. This is ethically questionable – although presumably from a poststructuralist position one can challenge the moral judgements on which concerns at misleading respondents are based. However, if our job as researchers is simply the production of stories (and, let's face it, stories which are composed in a far less entertaining or accessible style than those in the medium of popular fiction), one might ask whether we deserve our comparatively large salaries from the public purse. And of course, if research dissemination is simply story-telling, we have no way (or reason) to counter the conservative 'common-sense' knowledge about gender relations which, as Carrie Paechter points out in her chapter of this book, is already often used to reject 'expert' feminist positions.

I am unwilling to accept this relativist perception of the world, and of our work as researchers. The material actuality of our lives (for example, our sex, 'race', access to financial security and so on) inevitably impacts upon the ways in which we are positioned in discourse, and on our consequent power positions. And as I have pointed out previously (Francis 2001a; 2001b) we can and do form political allegiances in order to make social improvements (emancipatory projects). That the results of these endeavours may be somewhat limited and unpredictable does not necessarily mean that they are completely non-beneficial or worthless. The following section aims to explore some of the issues at stake here in greater detail.

Subjecthood, value and agency

The poststructuralist, anti-humanist view of the self has profound implications for research. As Hey (1999) observes, feminist researchers' conceptions of the establishment of rapport and empathy with respondents, and the gaining of a 'true' picture from them, are 'steeped in humanism'. Pattman et al. (1998) observe that many feminist researchers appear to retain a view of some respondent's answers (for example, where boys reveal their emotional vulnerability) as revealing an authentic, 'true' self. In contrast, Pattman et al. adopt a more postmodern position, rejecting the notion that a respondent's construction in one environment is more or less valid than her/his different construction in another. Hence they see boys' presentation of self in various situations (e.g. among the peer group, or speaking to an individual adult) as equally 'real' or 'unreal'.

So in regard to issues of value, agency, and the construction of the self, humanist feminism and relativist poststructuralism appear to stand in opposition. I have argued elsewhere that both perspectives on these issues are limited. Poststructuralist work has helped to deconstruct the humanist assumption that we are born with a complete, fixed personality which remains constant over time and in all social situations. People draw on different discourses and present themselves differently depending on the interactive environment (Francis 1998; 2000). And likewise, our power positions also fluctuate depending on the discursive environment. The humanist feminist position has consequently been revealed as often over-simplistic and unitary, with an inadequate recognition and explanation of the complexity of power relations. But these acknowledgements do not necessitate the conclusion that there is no coherence to our identities at all, or that we are without agency (Francis 2001a). The poststructuralist perspective cannot address trends of inequality, because it cannot be proscriptive: to recommend and/or work towards social improvement would involve the adoption of value-laden metanarratives. Moreover, poststructuralism potentially deconstructs the very notions of value and agency on which feminism is based.

I contend that neither humanist nor anti-humanist accounts of the self are representative of human action and experience. In my various discussions of this subject, I have suggested that in fact our 'personalities' express both inconsistency and consistency. I share the social constructionist view that we are not born with an essential personality intact. We develop our 'personalities', or construction of self, throughout our lives by drawing on the experiences and information around us, and this development is never completed. As social constructionists have long argued, our constructions of self depend on other people as well as ourselves: we construct and are constructed in social interaction. Yet I also suggest that some characteristics may be continually present in our 'personality' (although these too may develop over time), to the extent that those who 'know' us intimately may be able to predict our behaviour and responses to events quite accurately (Francis 2001a; 2002).

This complex picture of the self as reflecting continuity as well as inconsistency can be related to an account of agency which also acknowledges determinism. While poststructuralists see the self as positioned in (and determined by) discourse, Mills (1997) has argued that agency does not reside in discourses, but in people who can choose to utilize different discourses in order to position themselves and others in relations of power. Jones (1997) and Hood-Williams (1998) have argued that the assumption that we can choose which discourses to draw on is based on a humanist conception of the self. However, if we recognize that as well as being able to position ourselves and others through discourse we are simultaneously being positioned by others, and that such positioning is often beyond our control, this perspective can incorporate both agency and determinism. Cealey Harrison and Hood-Williams (2001) therefore maintain that this position resists relativism without wholly returning us to a humanist position.

The model of self which I am postulating, then, incorporates both contradiction and consistency; is constructed by the self her/himself and by others; and has agency but is also determined by material and discursive forces. It is an account which recognizes and (at least to some extent) accommodates the contradictory and complex nature of human interaction and power relations. Whilst clearly the account is as yet an embryonic one, requiring development, the next section reflects on the implications of this account of the self for the research process.

The research process and subjecthood

If there are consistencies as well as inconsistencies in our respondents' (and our own) presentations of self, can these ever be identified via the research process, and reported as 'fact'? I pointed out above that some of those close to us have often come to recognize trends and consistencies in our behaviour, enabling them to predict our behaviour with some accuracy (albeit this accuracy is never total). Of course, we do not usually 'know' our respondents to the extent required to judge the degree to which their responses are representative of their usual behaviour. Although their close friends might be able to do so, these friends are usually only familiar with the respondents' behaviour in particular environments. Hence one could never be confident that such judgements are representative of the respondents' 'total' presentation of self, nor of the 'authentic' model which notions of such 'knowledge' also imply, because as I have noted, there is no fixed person: we do often present ourselves differently in different environments (Francis 1998; 2001b). Hence while a respondent's school friends might 'know' her or him well enough to state whether a certain response is representative of the respondent's usual behaviour at school, this knowledge cannot necessarily be applied to other interactive environments. This is not to deny, however, that it remains the case that, even when we do not know respondents well, we can spot continuity as well as diversity in their presentation of self in different environments (Francis 2001b). I have discussed instances of such continuity among respondents in my own research (Francis 1998; 2000).

However, application of the position discussed above which rejects the humanist/anti-humanist dualism suggests that to ask whether a respondent's speech or behaviour represents 'the real' (authentic) person, and articulates a 'true' picture, is to ask the wrong questions. There is no stable, authentic person and as such there is no single 'true' reading of 'reality'. However, this does not mean that research cannot be useful or honest, or that our respondents' views and perspectives are not valid. Respondents are often passionately keen that their opinions and perceptions be articulated to and by the researcher. These opinions and perceptions are often, moreover, clearly deeply held (possibly reflecting foundational and relatively consistent aspects of the respondent's identity). For example, in my own research with young children, a few children were passionate in their rejection of gender stereotypical pigeon-holing of behaviour, and in their (often consistent) arguments against this (Francis 1998). To dismiss such contributions as fictions is, I think, disrespectful to respondents – and indeed to ourselves, who clearly hold some opinions and beliefs in a consistent way. So rather than asking if we are getting the 'real truth' from our respondents, we should instead be asking whether their responses can provide new insights with which to reflect on the subject of our research. For example, in my study, the children's passion about gender issues is intriguing in itself.

Further, reflexive research which attends conscientiously to issues of representation and validity, and openly declares the standpoint of the researcher (and hence the impact of her/his material and discursive position on what gets disseminated), can produce a truth. It is just that it is not the only, or a total, truth (Cealey Harrison 2001).

Such a shift in thinking does of course hold implications for our perception of specific issues during the research process. For example, there has been on-going debate as to whether respondent behaviour is affected by the presence of the researcher – generally it is accepted that the researchers' presence does have an impact. Seeing this as potentially distorting and invalidating the 'truth' which is disseminated as a result of the research, researchers often go to great lengths to minimize the apparent impact of their presence on the research environment. However, the perspective that I have outlined above highlights the point that there is no 'true' or 'authentic' behaviour to be 'found' by the researchers. Respondents' behaviour is no less 'real' or 'honest' due to the researchers' presence – it is simply more behaviour, one response in one interactive environment. And despite this, it remains interesting as human expression, and can provide useful insights for us as researchers to reflect upon and act upon. For example, that boys do say different things to their friends than to adult researchers (see above) is an important consideration. The differences in boys' construction of self depending on the interactive environment highlights the various social pressures and discourses they are negotiating in this production. And we as researchers remain free to speculate and theorize on the possible reasons for such difference.

This leads us back to the question of what we disseminate as research findings, highlighting my point about multiple truths. Because responses do change depending on the interactive environment, and because as researchers we bring our own constructions of self and reality to the research process, it is likely that different researchers will draw different findings from similar fields (or even from the same field). Such findings do not necessarily contradict each other: it is simply that different researchers often find different things of particular interest to focus on (Francis 2001b). One researcher might examine classroom behaviour according to gender and social class, and discover that boys of all social classes tend to dominate classroom space. But another researcher, examining the same research environment, might instead draw attention to the ways in which boys are underachieving in language subjects. Researchers are not omnipotent: one researcher will inevitably fail to notice, or fail to see the significance of, particular tendencies which another researcher might find pertinent and pick up. And such 'seeing' is inevitably influenced by the researchers' social position. This does not, however, invalidate all research. As I have said, research does not provide a totalizing truth about the fixed, authentic, 'real' world, because such a state does not exist, and so cannot be articulated. Good research simply disseminates a truth. That other truths may be found should be recognized in this dissemination.

As there has often been a concern for the respect of, and rapport with, respondents in traditional feminist research (see, for example, Skeggs 1994; Hey 1999), it is interesting to apply this argument about what our research 'finds' to the issue of the relationship between respondent and researcher, and to what is produced by this relationship. In the early research work inspired by second-wave feminism it tended to be assumed that women researchers and respondents could 'bond' together in shared experience and revelations, and that consequently a particularly valid, 'true' response was produced by respondents. During the period in which the feminist notion of a universal female subject was being challenged in the 1980s, concerns were raised as to whether, say, a white woman researcher could elicit a valid response from a black woman respondent. Edwards (1990) maintained that problems of difference (concerning, for example, ethnicity, social class, sexuality and so on) could be overcome by the allusion to and positioning in a shared womanhood between researcher and respondent. However, Phoenix (1987) challenged this argument, claiming that as black women and white women experience gender power relations differently due to the impact of racism in Western society, such power relations will inevitably impact on a black woman's responses to a white interviewer. However, the notion that black women researchers can gain 'authentic' responses from black women respondents has in turn been challenged by other writers. Feminists such as Mirza (1997) and Ang-Lygate (1996) have noted how the term 'black women' incorporates women from different religious, social class and ethnic groups (some of whom do not consider themselves 'black' at all). Hence it can be argued that the interview produced by, say, a middle-class Nigerian woman interviewer and a working-class African-Caribbean woman respondent may be no more valid than that of a middle-class white woman interviewer and a working-class African-Caribbean respondent. (Although it may be that the former couple may hold a shared experience of racism from the ethnic majority group which the latter couple lack.) Indeed, Mirza (1995) has shown how even when the interviewer shares the gender, ethnicity and religious background positioning with respondents, problematic differences can still arise and impact on responses and on the extent of 'empathy' formed between researcher and researched.

But from the position I have outlined above, which rejects the dualities of agency/determinism or the humanist/postmodern subject, we would expect people to produce themselves differently (to some extent) depending on the interviewer. As there is no single, stable, authentic expression of personhood, the different productions of self are all equally valid. However, if aspects of such presentation remain passionately articulated, or consistent across environments, these are interesting findings in themselves (as are silences and 'not saids'). And as Hey (1999) notes, moments of identification and empathy due to shared experience often do occur between the researcher and the respondent, yet not in a consistent or predictable way. Hey also observes that these points of recognition can be psychically painful as well as warm and/or enlightening.

It remains important, however, that we maintain an awareness that material differences between researcher and respondents (such as social class, ethnicity, age and so on) hold implications for our power positions in interaction, and on the response produced. I have outlined a theoretical position which assumes that people have agency (albeit limited), and can potentially apply political perspectives and other aspects of selfhood in relatively consistent ways. It therefore follows that feminist researchers are able to (and therefore should) endeavour to ensure that our respondents are not made to feel uncomfortable, intimidated or disempowered by the research process. We should not assume that we 'know' our respondents, or present their articulations to us as 'real' or 'total'. To do so is to violently reify one presentation of themselves at the expense of other possibilities, ignoring silences and power relations which have produced the 'not present'. But conversely, we may also find it interesting to note and to disseminate points of constancy as well as diversity in our respondents' presentation of themselves.

In this 'new agency' perspective, validity can still be maintained by ensuring that we do not over-generalize our findings, recognizing the limitations of our research, and by openly declaring the material factors which impact upon the perspective which we bring to bear on the world. Feminists are committed to a particular political view of the world, and this will (as they have traditionally recognized) inevitably impact on their research findings. A positivist view would suggest that such politically motivated research may be biased and 'un-objective' – yet as feminists have always argued, the conduct of *all* research is influenced by the researchers' 'standpoint'. The argument I have set out in this chapter demonstrates such concerns to be irrelevant, as there is no single 'true' picture to discover and disseminate. The account that we produce in disseminating the findings from rigorous research can be a 'true' one: however, it will inevitably represent only one of many truths, rather than being definitive and exclusive of others.

Finally, my position is not a completely relativist one. Although different researchers will find different points of interest and 'truths' from the same research environment, research does have a point – these various research findings are *not* simply fictions or stories. They represent the views and behaviour of respondents, however partially. It is for this reason that research work has been, and should continue to be, such a useful tool in the battle against gender-stereotypical and discriminatory assumptions and discourses which tend to work on the basis of fictions. A good example here is how feminist research in the classroom has consistently demonstrated the errors in popular assumptions that boys are now disadvantaged in the British education system. Dissemination is a valuable tool in feminist political work. However, as feminists we must remain sensitive, then, to the issues of nuance and power which are inevitably present in research and its dissemination, but which are often unarticulated. As good practice during our dissemination of research findings we ought to consider the issues of power at stake in our choice of *what* gets disseminated, and acknowledge that our dissemination is a partial, rather than total, 'truth'.

5 | Analysis or anecdote? Defending qualitative data before a sceptical audience

Chris Mann

Introduction

Qualitative research can offer insights into complex, multiple, even evolving truths. However, disseminating findings from studies that use qualitative methods can present great challenges to the researcher. Nowhere is this more problematic than when research has been conducted in hierarchical and/or bureaucratic institutions. This chapter charts the thinking of the author as she reflects on situations where she has had to defend qualitative data before a sceptical audience in such settings. This scepticism has been evoked not only by a methodological approach but also by a 'whiff of feminism' identified in her topics of research (which have tended to be within an equal opportunities framework with an emphasis on gender). And finally the scepticism has been triggered by something written on the body – a middle-aged woman trying to hold on to authenticity of personality and social class background in hierarchical masculinist settings.

Conducting qualitative research in institutions

Although there are many forms and uses of qualitative research, if there are new situations to deal with, or if an institution has intractable problems that do not seem to be explained by existing theories, qualitative research is stereotypically seen as the chosen method. This is because qualitative approaches enable the researcher to take an open-ended, exploratory approach where little is predefined or taken for granted. The hope would be that the researcher would look at the institution with a fresh eye, raising questions with regard to received wisdom, or introducing new ways of thinking. This, in turn, might challenge factors inhibiting positive policy change or suggest creative ways of going forward from which the institution would benefit.

However, the qualitative research process has implications for those in the institution and for the researcher. These implications may not be apparent to either until thorny issues of dissemination begin to surface.

Implications for institutional hierarchies

Historically, qualitative research has tended to focus on the relatively *powerless* rather than the social elites found in powerful organizations or the state apparatus. Hence the emphasis may be on those 'over whom power is exercised rather than societies' decision makers' (Odendahl and Shaw 2002: 299). However, a researcher may successfully gain access to elites as part of an overall investigation into an institution. A key element of much qualitative research is that it attempts to understand experience within a context taken as a whole. The researcher who wants to find out what makes people tick in their own world needs to look at all aspects of the interactions they are involved in. Thus, within institutions, the search for a holistic picture may encompass those at the top of the hierarchy as well as the less powerful. As qualitative research looks deeply into social patterns, attempting to understand the concepts, behaviours, perceptions and accounts of all informants, this may involve attempts to penetrate the closed structures which characterize elite groups (Hertz and Imber 1995). This is always a challenge, which is why there is very little extant research looking exclusively at elites.

> The privileges and responsibilities of elites are often not tangible or transparent, making their world difficult to penetrate. Sometimes, a cloak of privacy, or even secrecy, masks their activities.
>
> (Odendahl and Shaw 2002: 299)

Given the responsibilities that powerful people may have to the organization as a whole, it is not surprising that they may initially refuse any risk to themselves by denying or limiting access to their world. Unfortunately, even if a researcher is allowed access, this does not imply that a research project can be fully executed. A skilled qualitative researcher may evoke a considerable amount of information from powerful members of organizations. Indeed, if the researcher has been underestimated (and qualitative researchers frequently are) informants may speak candidly because they discount the researcher's 'capacity to do much with the information' (Odendahl and Shaw 2002: 312). However, once the analysis of data is complete, this complacency may prove unfounded.

It can become clear that the researcher might, after all, pose a threat to the establishment. Elite groups are often sensitive to the way their image is portrayed and may start to see a researcher as 'a relatively uncontrollable element in an otherwise highly controlled system of bureaucracy' (Renzetti and Lee 1993: 9). Apart from the risk of 'losing face', or the fear of upsetting the status quo, some elite groups may also fear that an open-minded researcher may impose an implicit threat to the *culture* of the organization itself – an organization whose rules and discipline may provide a source of identity for its members (Renzetti and Lee 1993). Of course, if elite groups are using power within organizations in a dubious or illegitimate manner, or in a way that outsiders might construe in such negative terms, they will see insightful researchers as an obvious liability. In these circumstances even those who had initially supported, even initiated, investigations within an institution may intervene at the final stage of the research to control the dissemination of critical findings. Indeed, even when the findings seem fairly anodyne, the participation of elite groups in research seems to make processes of dissemination more complex and restricted than they would have been otherwise.

Powerful people have a range of ways to deflect or undermine dissemination. Renzetti and Lee (1993) point out that elite groups are usually articulate and self-confident, with sufficient power, resources and expertise to protect their reputation. Powerful groups are often characterized by intricate interpersonal networks that include influential actors behind the scenes (Odendahl and Shaw 2002). These networks can 'dampen down' the research process in different ways. They may find ways to slow down or dissipate the dissemination process; may suppress or substantially modify the accounts researchers have given of their activities (Adler and Adler 1993); and they may move to throw doubt on a researcher's motives, methods and credibility (Renzetti and Lee 1993).

It is not surprising that many researchers balk at the thought of disseminating findings from a study which includes critical comment on the affairs of power-holders. Apart from the possibility of interventions to block or undermine the research, they will also be aware that influential organizations have very sophisticated 'positive sanctions' at their disposal. At a practical level elites may well have in their gift both funding for research and the key to future career openings. Where the researcher is directly employed by the institutional elite, it will also be these groups who pay the mortgage and who have the authority to call their 'employee' to account.

Dealing with bureaucratic institutions

When large institutions set up research projects there is often a substantial period between initiating the research and the results being ready – this is particularly the case in qualitative research, where both data collection and analysis can be time-consuming. In the meantime there may be a turnover of personnel or a change of attitude towards the research. In some cases, the mere fact of the project being started is enough to quell institutional unrest over particular sensitive issues – giving a feeling that they have been dealt with. The emergence of results is not always seen as a positive development in such situations. Alternatively, the actual (though unstated) motive of those setting up the research may have been simply to show that 'something is being done', with no real expectation that serious and policy-influencing results might materialize from it. Challenging findings in these circumstances are rarely welcome.

In either case there can be a problem that, as time has gone by, the initiators of the research have moved on. The composition of elite groups in organizations is often relatively fluid and changes over time (Odendahl and Shaw 2002: 299) and new managers may not be clear about why there was such urgency about setting up the project in the first place. People further down the pecking order who have been delegated the responsibility for monitoring the progress of the research – and who may not have been the keen individuals who first set it in motion – will be left with overseeing the dissemination of the report. In this kind of circumstance individuals and groups may not know what to do with the material they are presented with, and may not have the authority to disseminate it effectively.

Large bureaucratic institutions may also be very amateurish when it comes to dissemination. Unless there is a strong overall strategy, a long qualitative report may simply be set on the shelf because no one is able (or willing) to take responsibility for its dissemination. Groups can work with the material in a very ad hoc way as they veer between their sense of responsibility for dealing with the findings they are presented with, and the very human response, particularly if the findings are critical, of thinking 'do we really need this now – is it really necessary?' There is a particular difficulty if the organizational structure of the institution is based on committees. Without an overall lead from a key person, it is hard for a committee to take responsibility for moving research results forward (particularly if they are critical). Sometimes it is unclear who has the authority to make decisions about the form and content of the results which should be presented to insiders and/or outsiders. As always with committees, it may be hard to settle on a joint strategy and procrastination can seem the 'safest pair of hands'. There can also be a terror of leaks as the findings make their slow and stately way through the different levels of the hierarchy, and there may be a temptation to place ever-increasing restrictions on the material which can be released beyond a small inner circle.

Where does this leave the researcher? Some committees take the dissemination out of the hands of the researcher completely and decide to handle affairs on their own. In this situation the researcher may only hear about the progress of the report by hearsay; the road between 'submission of final report' and 'dissemination of findings' may be long, with movement (if any) very difficult to track. This kind of assimilation of the researcher's work by the institution can lead to various kinds of marginalization. Is the author's name clearly on the cover? Or is tucked in a footnote while the logo of the company or institution rides high above the work – and does it matter? What if committee members choose to be the 'front people' who discuss the work in face-to-face sessions with others in the institution without the researcher being present? What assurance does the researcher have that the methodology and findings are being portrayed in a way that reflects the researcher's ideas and beliefs? How can researchers defend their methodology before a possibly sceptical audience if they are not even present? In a worst case scenario, how can the researcher challenge individuals, ostensibly speaking on their behalf, who may be deliberately rubbishing the work for reasons linked to their own career agenda?

These are clearly problematic areas and bring home the realization that researchers need to give a lot of thought to contractual agreements about dissemination. The pattern in the US, where litigation seems a more active possibility than in many parts of Europe, is for contracts to be quite precise. In contrast, the default form of many social science contracts in the UK seems to focus on a simple exchange of fair payment for work produced within a given amount of time. In some situations there may be a clause stating that findings must remain within the institution and not enter the public domain and this helps clarify whether the intellectual property rights belong to the commissioning institution or the researcher. However, in situations where the legal contract *does not* specify whether researchers have sufficient ownership of their work to warrant having a clear voice in the dissemination of findings, problems lie ahead. The form of dissemination (is it oral and in what form?, is it written and in what form?, is it interactive, possibly discussed in a meeting or on a web page or, is it non-reactive, even 'authorless'?); the site of dissemination (are findings found in academic journals, press releases, institutional reports, on the Internet?); the scope of dissemination (is it detailed findings, an overview, limited sections?); the extent of dissemination (is it open to all, restricted to a few, lost without trace?); the nature of the disseminator (does the researcher take personal responsibility for disseminating findings or do other 'players' take over?) – all these questions and more tend to be skirted over until the end of the research process. At that stage, an organization may be pulling one way about dissemination and the researcher the other. Without a clear contract a researcher who has different ideas from the institution might be left struggling with the ethics of disseminating material independently. Only when agreement is reached at the outset of the work can researchers feel able to express the resolution shown in the following quote.

> Whereas compromise in terms of timing of the release of publications may sometimes be necessary, the researcher should not compromise

the integrity of the work by allowing elites to have a voice in deciding what is published and where.

(Ostrander 1995: 149)

That being said, researchers who do not work as part of large, experienced and influential research centres may feel very unsure about how to set down ground rules at the beginning of a project. It can be hard to know who to negotiate terms with, and who to challenge if formal or informal understandings of processes end up at cross-purposes. Clearly more work needs to be done in this area.

Dealing with dissemination as a qualitative researcher

It is too easy as a qualitative researcher to forget that the research methods you use are a mystery to many people, including, quite possibly, those responsible for overseeing your research or hoping to learn from it. Even with the best will in the world, individuals may be unsure about what you are doing, why it is taking so long, and why you have so little to show in the way of firm conclusions at milestones along the way. It is one thing to convince a research committee that has been given the responsibility of appointing you about the value of your methods. It is another thing to convince other members of the institution that has employed you once they hear about the research you are doing.

In one study I was involved in, a high-status member of the institution asked me to prepare a report for a 'progress' meeting. He wanted me to deliver a presentation explaining what qualitative research was, how it worked in practice, and how it would work in the study in question. This colleague had a strong background in positivist research methods in a non-social science subject and was genuinely mystified about qualitative methodology. It was a pleasure to prepare this material both in itself, and because I could see that it would be a useful dry run before wider dissemination of the material to other sceptics. They would be, perhaps, less open to learning about the methodology, particularly if the findings it had generated were seen as critical. In retrospect I think I went overboard on this presentation, perhaps thinking I could bring everyone 'on side' about qualitative research, so ensuring that my future results would be seen as valid by even the most sceptical in the institution. In the event I concluded that most people would be more likely to recognize the value in what a qualitative researcher has done if, in the end, the researcher manages to:

present the experience of the people that he or she interviews in compelling enough detail and in sufficient depth that those who read the study can connect to that experience, learn how it is constituted, and deepen their understanding of the issues it reflects.

(Seidman 1991: 41)

Of course, it is not usually possible to present a really convincing progress report until the qualitative research is at an advanced stage. At an early point in one of my research projects I prepared 'discussion papers' for a project management committee. The committee had been given the task of meeting me on a regular basis to make sure the work I was employed to do was successfully completed. The discussion papers I presented to the group included discursive narratives that drew on textual material I had generated up to that point in the research. As a qualitative researcher I presented this material as 'work in progress' rather than 'first findings'. I was trying to engage the readers in the complex areas that were emerging and to flag the issues that they might care to discuss with me if they found them interesting. The response of many of those present was salutary. They were totally bemused by the material and looked in vain for titles, sub-titles, bullet points and executive overviews. I realized that I had unfairly expected this group to function as brainstorming facilitators who would play an active part in formulating analysis. It was clear that, in an institutional context, I would be expected to find user-friendly ways to disseminate early 'conclusions' to colleagues. Although I attempted to do this at later meetings I was always wary that some points would be seized upon and remembered simply because they were positive in tone, even if these points would be contra-dicted by further information as the analysis continued.

Dissemination: the written report

As noted above, qualitative research may be less familiar to many people than more statistical studies, and in certain contexts there may be a serious level of scepticism about the methodology. The reservations about qualita-tive research colour many aspects of the reception that greets written reports of findings.

The size of the report

As a qualitative researcher I usually include a great deal of textual data. But while I see this as an essential part of communicating findings I am forced to recognize that many 'readers' of the report will skip this material. This is partly because individuals want to see summary statistics, not 'waffle'. In the words of one person who had to read a rather copious report that I had written: 'once you've read the juicy bits it's just a lot of chat really'. How-ever, even those who may wish to read the material rarely have time to do so. This is a serious problem. It is salutary when even the most concerned indi-viduals may contact you to say, 'I just haven't time to get to grips with all of this – which bits should I definitely read?'

The size of some qualitative reports has other implications. It can be expensive to produce in a professional manner for dissemination purposes. While many statistically based reports appear in glossy folders, qualitative work can be relegated to amateurish printouts that save institutions money. Further, if written reports seem too large, too wordy or even too physically heavy to be disseminated to everyone there may an executive decision to break up the report and to send different parts to different splinter groups. While this is an obviously practical solution, there is the danger that it can be used as a strategy to control dissemination, with certain groups seeing less and others more of the less palatable findings.

There are other drawbacks. Time spent reading long reports can lead to a delay in the dissemination of findings beyond elite groups. Those outside these groups who hope to bring about policy change might find that vital deadlines offering such opportunities have passed before they have essential information at their fingertips. Doubt can also be cast on findings by the suggestion that, by the time the report is released, the data are out of date and 'the situation has changed'. The delay can also have a negative effect on the researcher's progressing career. It is sometimes difficult, if not impossible, to move to new projects if the research is moving at a snail's pace to the public domain and there is no possibility of producing papers because the only message that comes through loud and clear is 'don't speak out yet – we don't want any leaks yet'.

The question 'what is to be done with all those words?' has to be addressed. It could be argued that qualitative reports would benefit in every way from being made shorter, and there is no doubt that executive reports and a clear, attractive 'at a glance' presentation of key findings is crucial. But while bullet points work very well in statistical reports where they can be backed up by numbers, they look pretty thin and unconvincing in reports of qualitative research without the textual data which supports them (or even with quotes in a truncated form). The problem is that qualitative findings develop from a net of interconnecting factors, some of which are very subtle and only surface in what some people see as a textual ramble. People who only receive the executive summary would be quite justified in asking: 'how do you defend this conclusion?' – and unlike statistics where you can say 'I did this test', with qualitative research you have no choice but to say 'I generated this data and it said this and that'.

Including statistics in qualitative reports

Some qualitative research projects use qualitative and quantitative work in an iterative way so that each aspect of the research process informs the other. In many studies this is a very fruitful way of working, but the way in which a report is formulated may give stronger emphasis to either one or the other method. A report that emphasizes statistical findings will often use qualitative material in an illustrative way, reproducing one or two telling comments to back up the force of the numerical patterns. A report written by a qualitative researcher gives much less emphasis to the numbers. The researcher may introduce statistics to give general patterns or to show the boundaries of context, but the numbers will not drive the qualitative analysis. I have written strongly qualitative reports in which I have been told to 'distance' myself from statistics I have included at the point of dissemination because the statistical tests 'lack sophistication'. It is in vain for a qualitative researcher to protest that sophisticated statistical tests usually demand large numbers, and that qualitative research will rarely be dealing with large numbers. In the worst scenarios, influential members of the institution may insist that, for dissemination purposes, different categories of people are grouped together in order to give 'overall patterns'. The qualitative researcher will then be faced with trying to defend their carefully disaggregated material (which is attempting to show the subtlety of a situation) from being slung together in a new 'useful' category which will enable more complex statistical tests to be run, so producing results which lose the sensitivity of the qualitative analysis – and in some cases undermine it.

Dissemination: the verbal report

Qualitative researchers are often asked to defend their 'anecdotal' findings in person to frequently sceptical individuals and groups. In institutional settings the skills and personal attributes which may make someone a good intuitive researcher may be the very social and personal characteristics which make the researcher the worst possible disseminator of their own material. For me, as a middle-aged, working-class woman, to present a verbal report in, for instance, an elite, male-dominated institution can be counterproductive. Contexts of privilege, where the atmosphere is of unquestioned and unquestioning superiority, may be intimidating. In some environments accents and speech patterns are picked up as if by radar and lightning judgements are made. People may not be able to guess immediately that my ancestors were peasants who fled the potato famine in Ireland for work in the docks of Liverpool. But they recognize at once that I did not go to private school; that I do not have the bearing of the aristocrat; that I do not carry my hard-won academic status with innate confidence and gravitas. When I disseminate findings in person, it is difficult to quell my tendency to be unfashionably 'smiley' or to respond to any feeling of being subtly put down with the 'cheekiness' which is the legacy of my early brushes with authority. I am also constitutionally unable to talk in jargon or to quote impressive-sounding theories that I think are pretentious, or to separate what I think from what I feel. It is clearly a challenge for someone like me, whose face and whole demeanour may hit the wrong note, to defend qualitative research in person to sceptics.

Yet it is my background and life experience which have made me passionate about equal opportunities, and which have sensitized me to the narratives and accounts of those whose voices are rarely heard. In many situations I have a personal investment in informing policy change and helping to bring about increasingly equitable environments. What lessons must I learn to disseminate effectively?

Getting the message across

The advice that is generally offered to researchers who want to make a difference is to distance themselves from their beliefs in order to take a 'neutral' position. But is this position neutral? I have been told that studies I cite within institutions should be 'mainstream' (i.e. not feminist work) or it will increase the amused indifference with which qualitative work will be greeted in many circles. With written reports for elites I have been told to avoid all pejorative words such as 'prejudice' or 'oppressive' as I will be considered inflammatory and 'hysterical'. Yet in other settings and with different audiences, concepts and experiences that seem challenging, even combative, are recognized as authentic ways of seeing and describing the world. The conclusion I have reached is that researchers who wish to be effective do need to write multiple reports, and to make presentations which are tailored to different audiences. Formality, vocabulary, even the ways in which findings are described may need to vary. For instance, in some contexts it is more effective to discuss findings in terms of the experiences of 'lower orders' and not the elite. Even so, the alert reader is able to read between the lines and see that the experiences of one are symbiotically linked to the actions of the other.

These compromises are made because it is often the elite groups who have initiated the research – and they generally have the power to make policy changes. There is also no point in thinking 'publish and be damned' if you actually *are* damned in terms of undermining the possibility of bringing about change by antagonizing institutions and making them defensive. Disseminating research is a sensitive business and it is often a good idea to play a long game. For instance, at MIT the women's faculty in science demonstrated to the Dean of the School of Science that there were indeed unjustified inequalities for women in the institution.

> The problem was that the data that convinced the Dean were highly confidential. The original report outlined in great detail, department by department, personal material that was very private, often embarrassing, and no one wanted it to be made public. After a number of revisions that were still not publishable, we decided on a narrative report of what had happened, how it came about and how the Dean responded. Our intent was to inform the MIT faculty, but when the

report hit the front page of the New York Times, it informed a much wider audience.

(Bailyn 2001: 10)

A lesson to be learned from the MIT experience is that careful dissemination can still result in wide exposure but without the knock-back effects of treating findings in a sensationalist way or being naïvely trusting about the part the press might play. By making sure the press focused on the research process, broad rather than intrusive findings, and the enlightened response of a power-holder within the institution (the Dean) to these findings, the MIT women ensured that everyone involved in the study was seen in a positive light. By portraying the research process in this upbeat manner the way was open for constructive policy change without the baggage of recrimination and defensiveness from those involved.

At the same time the researcher will have in mind those for whom findings from the research will have most impact. In hierarchical institutions it is often those who are at the bottom of the pecking order who have the greatest hopes of benefiting should change come about, but they are often the last to know what's going on. In one educational establishment in which I worked, the focus of the research was on the experiences of undergraduates, but results were disseminated from the centre of an immensely complicated power network with the Vice-Chancellor and close associates at the core, branching out to ever-widening circles of academic, administrative and pastoral committees. Apart from several official student representatives at these committees (who had to treat the information as fully confidential) there was a long distance to be travelled before any 'student on the campus' might be party to research findings, even though many of them had contributed to the study and it focused on their own well-being.

In situations such as this it is not only a matter of ensuring that findings are eventually disseminated widely but of making sure that they are presented in a user-friendly way. In research in which the researcher is not constrained by the structures of funding bodies or employers, dissemination can be a creative process in which the medium is the message. I have disseminated my findings in chats in coffee bars, as email attachments to interested colleagues worldwide, through student newspapers, as case studies in training courses, in discussion with practitioner friends, and when teaching or giving pastoral advice to individual students. In some settings the commitment to and passion about my work, which is seen as a worrying sign of possible bias in some quarters, is taken as additional evidence to support the validity of my findings. Qualitative researchers who believe in their work are often most effective at disseminating their material in small groups of genuinely interested and/or concerned people. It is in this kind of interactive setting that research studies can be discussed at depth with the possibility of generating transformative understanding of the issues.

We are less likely to know how our formal non-interactive reports will be 'heard' by others. The literature on dissemination seems to assume that we can know who will read our material and we can control how they assimilate our ideas. In fact, in a knowledge society where we are swamped with information, we do not, and cannot, know how what we have written is taken up. In one study I was involved in, the high achievement of particular groups of university students was linked with pre-university participation in extra curricula activities organized by high-powered networks of experts and enthusiasts in the subject area. The point I made in my report was that such groups could increase inequity by marginalizing those who did not have the knowledge or the finance or the social backing to take part in these activities. In the event some readers of the report contacted me, not about the implications of this finding, but to ask me how a young person could join the specialized groups. Another problem is that, with the best will in the world, it is difficult to avoid having words we write read in terms of stereotypes. In a journal article, I discussed how teaching and learning processes help construct women and girls as low in confidence and dependent for success on hard work, and men and boys as intellectual risk-takers (Mann 2002). Yet I wonder whether this analysis will, in fact, be used to support the received wisdom I am trying to deconstruct. To make sense of what I am saying the reader would have to follow the nuances of the argument. Unless people are prepared to invest time in reading the full text of the article the gender stereotypes seem to remain.

As we do not know how our words will be read, all we can do is make an educated guess about some of the dangers of being misrepresented and try to take steps to avoid sounding ambiguous. A crisp, succinct, well-argued report that appears in the public domain will be worth its weight in gold to those who need to convince others of their cause, and researchers who can provide material of this kind may find that others will continue the dissemination process they started. Apart from anything else, they give the less powerful the 'acceptable' evidence they need to work for change.

The quality of qualitative research

Do these reflections on disseminating qualitative research conform with the view that such research is guilty, as often charged, of being irrelevant to the wider community because its studies are often small-scale and non-generalizable? This has not been my experience. In circumstances where dissemination processes allow the immediacy of the data to be transmitted there can be a startled, almost 'time stood still' recognition of shared experience; experience that is felt to be similar in essence regardless of differences in context and personnel.

In the course of one study I disseminated findings about student learning styles at a large conference. My presentation included a number of extensive student quotes that illustrated the unfolding analysis. At the conclusion of the talk a professor from a prestigious science institution offered the view that 'People in science dismiss educational theory. But if they could have been here today and seen this material – the strength and authenticity of it – they could not help but be convinced.' He suggested that I went round science faculties such as his own and used my Powerpoint presentations to introduce the qualitative material to those most sceptical of audiences – staff teaching the natural sciences. They, when faced with apparent 'anecdotes' would, he assured me, recognize them as analysis because, as noted in Seidman (1991: 41) cited above, they would 'connect' to those experiences and by so doing would deepen their understanding of the issues they reflected.

6 | Intricacies of dissemination in ethnographic research
Tuula Gordon

Dissemination in ethnography

This chapter explores issues of dissemination in relation to an ethnographic project that I, and five colleagues, have recently been engaged in. This project on 'Citizenship, Difference and Marginality in Schools – with Special Reference to Gender' involved six of us participating in everyday life at school for the duration of one school year (with subsequent follow-up) in two secondary schools in Helsinki. We started our fieldwork on the first school day, attached to 7th grade classes of 13–14 year old students new to the school (Gordon et al. 1999; Lahelma and Gordon 1997). Alongside them we began to find our way round the school, trying to learn the appropriate time-space paths, getting to know the classes we were attached to, as well as the teachers who taught those classes. Dissemination was a relevant issue right from the beginning. We have worked closely with Janet Holland, who has conducted similar research in two secondary schools in London (Gordon, Holland and Lahelma 2000). Although many issues in respect of dissemination were shared between the Helsinki and London teams, specific issues had to be addressed in the Finnish context, and I limit my discussion to those experiences as well as discussing pertinent issues in ethnographic research in general. Ethics and politics of dissemination confront the researcher in an intertwined manner both in the field and in publishing.

In ethnographic research, questions about dissemination begin when entry is negotiated. We had to describe our project when we negotiated our entry into schools. We addressed audiences of teachers in two schools, trying to convince the staff of each school that our project was interesting and worthwhile, and why. And from the first day onwards in City Park and in Green Park, as we call our schools, we had to answer questions – the most prevalent being 'what are you doing here?'.

We have been trying to disseminate in a range of ways, in a range of contexts, often collectively, and often in close discussion with the people we are disseminating to. Inevitably, therefore, the whole process is very complex and ongoing in the context of ethnography. For example, we have had to think about the ways in which we use our data to illustrate our analysis in writing, in seminars, in conferences – as well as in our teaching. What do we tell? How much do we tell? What do we not tell? How do we find the correct style of combining an analytical approach as well as more pedagogic and political content? Whilst we take these concerns very seriously, there is no doubt that dissemination sometimes causes pain – to us as researchers as well as to those who participate in our research.

In Finland, educational politics and policies are keenly discussed. Comprehensive education has been considered to have important social relevance in the quest for an egalitarian welfare state. However, New Right policies have sharpened differentiation, for example through increasing movement from local 'ordinary' schools to schools with higher academic reputations (although differences between schools are smaller than in Britain, for example). Because of the more comprehensive, democratic structure of education (Gordon, Holland and Lahelma 2000) schooling is of important public, social and political concern. Educational research is more likely to be publicly discussed in Finland than in many other places.

Ethnography in schools

In the project we have been interested in constructions of difference in schools. Our starting point is gender, but we see gender as intersecting with other differences of social class, 'race', ethnicity, sexuality and impairment, and all formed the basis for our observations and the multiple methods of data collection we employed. We are interested in how processes of differentiation and marginalization in schools produce the citizen of the nation state and how agency and subjectivity are forged in these processes. The broader educational terrain is contextualized through an analysis of New Right politics and policies in education and their relationship to equal opportunity politics.

In developing our conceptual and theoretical framework we have drawn freely on a range of theoretical perspectives, including social constructionist, cultural, materialist, poststructural and feminist theory. Our aim is to theorize individuals as agents with subjectivities in the production of society as well as to consider material constraints and possibilities with which society confronts the individual (Gordon, Holland and Lahelma 2000).

Once funding for the project was secured from the Academy of Finland, we had to get in touch with the local Department of Education in order to obtain permission to do research in schools. We looked for particular types of school: one more working class, the other more middle class; one in the central area, the other in the suburbs; one school in a new building, the other in an old building. We did not want a stark contrast between the schools. We had decided to include two schools in the study because we wanted a certain amount of variation. But the second reason was dissemination – we felt that we were better able to preserve anonymity of the schools, teachers, students and other staff, if we had two schools. We had therefore considered dissemination of our written texts even before we were in the field. We then chose potential schools and visited several of them. We spoke to head teachers first, and then talked about our research to teachers, who had an opportunity to ask questions and to express their worries. We managed to negotiate entry for long-term research in two schools that fitted our criteria well.

We observed these schools for one school year, conducted interviews and collected a range of data. We followed form groups and conducted observation and participant observations during lessons, breaks and special events. Our observations were based on a jointly planned non-structured list of foci based on previous, exploratory school visits (Gordon 1993). Our participant observations were recorded in field diaries at the end of each day. We interviewed students, teachers and other staff, and collected association and metaphors, as well as using questionnaires. After this one school year we visited the schools intermittently. Elina (co-researcher) and I have now started to trace the transitions of these young people, and have interviewed 63 of them again at the ages of 17–18 and are currently conducting second follow-up interviews at the ages of 19–20.

On the third day the students of the class I was attached to in City Park started asking more closely who I was and why I was in the school. During the first couple of days the students had been so concerned to find their own place in the school that they had not paid a great deal of attention to me.

> [The students] have started to ask more intensely what I am doing. Suddenly several of them came to enquire. Therefore we decided that I shall talk to them about the research during one lesson. I explained at the end of the lesson – Pirkko was there with me [. . .] I emphasised confidentiality and that we were, sort of, in a similar situation as they and that although we move between students and teachers we will not carry any stories from one to the other. They listened. Unfortunately there was no time for questions.
>
> (Tuula Gordon, Diary 18.8)

This attempt to provide information about the research sparked further questions. The students want to know more details.

> The students would like to know where the other research school is. [. . .] I gather courage and ask if our presence bothers them. Lotta says that it is nice and few other girls seem to agree. I'm really relieved.
>
> (Tuula Gordon, Diary 25.8)

The students are particularly interested in our field notes.

> At the end of the lessons students came to count how many pages of notes I had written. They try to read my notes, but luckily enough they cannot decipher my handwriting.
>
> (Tuula Gordon, Diary 5.9)

> Ella asks me if I will write down that they were late. [. . .] Lotta asks me if I write down everything they say.
>
> (Tuula Gordon, Diary 15.9)

We also have to talk about research at parents' evenings.

> I introduce our research. Many of them seem to have heard about it. Nods and smiles when I explain who I am.
>
> (Tuula Gordon, Diary 12.9)

Ethnographers depend on the kindness of strangers, as Christopher Wellin and Gary Alan Fine (2001) suggest. Many ethnographers in organizations have to negotiate with organizational gatekeepers (Smith 2000). We had conducted our initial negotiations with the head teachers, but having entered the schools, we found that we needed to keep renegotiating entry into specific situations in the school, such as particular lessons, special events and discussions. In that sense the everyday life at school is a field full of gatekeepers. We might be welcomed to a lesson, but this did not guarantee that students or teachers had the time or inclination to discuss the project with us. The researcher in the field is constantly 'in-between' (Tolonen 2001: 46–7). We were constantly explaining what we were doing and why; we had to have a tale to tell about our research, concise and clear enough to be told repeatedly: who we were, what we were interested in, what our methods were and exactly what we would do in the school. There was often ambivalence about what should or could be included in this tale. Ethnographic researchers study localized cultures – whilst doing so, they are constantly filtering these cultures through their own selves. As Wellin and Fine suggest, 'being dependent on informants' consent fosters empathy, as well as ambiguous obligations of reciprocity' (Wellin and Fine 2001: 323).

We have suggested that studying schools provides rich material to surprise and to startle; accounts can be rendered in a gripping style of semi-warfare. We have tried to focus on stories of cooperation as well as on stories of conflict. We do not see teachers as agents of the state, with a sole interest in control, and every limitation is for us, as for Giddens (1985), an opportunity for enactment. We frame the events in our schools in the context of politics and policies. We try to materialize the cultural order we have observed, and the patterns of interaction which constitute that order. Our main focus is on gender, but we have tried to take difference seriously; we are constantly talking about students as gendered and belonging to particular groups, and then disentangling these constructions to think about them from a different perspective (Gordon, Holland and Lahelma 2000; Gordon, Hynninen, Metso, Lahelma, Palmu and Tolonen, 2000).

We engage in critical educational research, whereby the main edge of our criticism is directed towards educational politics and policies. Our aim has been to demonstrate how these materialize, albeit in diverse, complex ways, in everyday life at school. Our aim was not to engage in criticism of individual people in the school, neither students nor teachers.

Metaphor struggle

Despite our careful preparation, we encountered a dissemination drama relatively early on. During the spring of our fieldwork year I received a telephone call at seven in the morning from the head teacher in City Park, our other research school. 'Good morning, I'm phoning from the madhouse'. My response was bewildered. The head teacher explained that she had read about our research in the main Finnish daily newspaper that morning. I rang off and read the paper, where I found a headline: 'School is a prison, a madhouse and a factory'. In the Gender and Education researchers' network, prior to our research, we had conducted a collective exercise on the school in question. We had visited schools and observed space, embodiment, movement, time and voice. We had conducted a brief metaphor questionnaire, our aim being to chart the implications of space. The questionnaire had four questions: 'What places do you like in the school?', 'What places do you dislike?', 'How do you spend your breaks?' and finally, 'Complete the sentence: School is like . . .'. We were interested whether this last question would produce references to space. The data was full of negative metaphors, many of them referring to total institutions. We decided to conduct our analysis on the school using these metaphors. We wrote an article about them in the *Finnish Youth Research Journal* (Gordon, Lahelma and Tolonen 1995; see also Gordon and Lahelma 1996). A journalist had picked that up and wrote about it in the daily newspaper, in somewhat sensational terms. There is a difference in saying school 'is a jail' as the newspaper report quoted us, or saying school is '*like* a jail' as we wrote in our article. We then suggested that metaphors reveal and clarify one story, whilst hiding other stories, for example, the pleasure involved in informal interaction in school. We concluded that rigid time-space paths in schools gave students scant agency, and the negative metaphors picked up on that.

We had to rush to the school to provide our explanations, write letters to all the teachers, a letter to the newspaper, and a letter to the teachers' trade union journal. Our relations with the research schools were patched, although we had inadvertently angered, and also upset, a large number of teachers.

In the end the metaphor debacle served some positive ends. It was tied up with discussions about what sort of environments schools were. But it also demonstrated difficulties of dissemination. Being engaged in critical research and disseminating to our colleagues means that different kinds of messages may be sent to those in the field. It is time-consuming to deal with these questions.

Dialogue and reciprocity in research

We had hoped to have dialogue with teachers and students, and a certain amount of reciprocity, whilst our main cooperative collective consisted of the research group. The time-space paths of the teachers in Finnish upper secondary school are tight, so it was unlikely that we could engage in intensely cooperative research with them. However, we were trying to engage in dialogue. But dialogue was difficult primarily because of time constraints, but also because we addressed somewhat different issues than teachers, and thirdly because of the critical stance we adopted. The critical stance was aimed, first of all, at educational politics and policies and the New Right restructuring of education. Secondly, the critical stance was aimed at the school as an institution, its rigidity and its hierarchy. Our aim was not to be critical of our research schools, their teachers, students or other people we came in contact with. But as these schools served as instances of 'the school' for us, it has always been difficult to distinguish these aims. We did not want to harm our research schools – or teachers, students and other staff in them – in any way. Moreover, we hoped that they, as well as a broader audience of researchers, educational administrators and teachers would benefit from our work (Murphy and Dingwall 2000).

In practice I have written, jointly with Janet Holland and Elina Lahelma, about our four research schools – two in Helsinki and two in London – in ways that often leaves them undifferentiated. Our aim, for example, was to develop an analysis of spatial praxis in schools; we were concerned to develop more general theorization about spatiality. But of course it would have been interesting to differentiate more clearly between specific practices in these four schools. This, however, we did not want to do. Our commitment to anonymity and ethics has been very strong. There have been times when we have omitted pseudonyms or changed them. We have blurred some background data and changed some background circumstances.

Yet dialogue was constantly ongoing in the field, sometimes in an intense manner, sometimes with a sense of discomfort as an intruder. The relationship between teachers, students and researchers is one of reciprocity; we could not be mere observers even if we would have wanted to. There were times during fieldwork when we felt our interactional skills were stretched to the limit, not least because we were between students and teachers and therefore traversing clearly marked positions in the school.

We have sent a selection of our academic work to the schools. But further difficulty is found here. Researchers work slowly, whereas teachers wanted quicker results. We had a great deal of data, as is typical for ethnographic research. We tried to meet the teachers' wishes by writing brief reports to teachers in each of our schools, as well as to the students in our classes. For the students these at least served as a memory of their engagement in the research. For the teachers I suspect their expectations were not met. The initial results we disseminated to teachers were far too superficial to engage their concerns; we were not able to do justice to our vast data, the analysis of which was just beginning. We have, finally, written a report aimed at teachers and other practitioners in education (Lahelma and Gordon, forthcoming). We disseminated the report to the schools prior to its publication. We decided that the report should be accessible to as many teachers as possible. Therefore some teachers found the discussions rather obvious. Whilst we were careful not to engage in writing that would be inaccessible and overly critical, aspects of our report nevertheless irritated some teachers. Others found useful the ways in which 'voice' and 'space' are approached, and they had started to focus more on such issues.

Teachers have also read some of our 'academic' publications, but for them it is problematic that a great deal of our writing is in English, and therefore less accessible. There are several reasons for publishing in English. We want to communicate with non-Finnish-speaking researchers focusing on gender and education and/or conducting ethnographic research. In order to do so we have to write in English. Secondly, there is an expectation in Finland that researchers publish internationally in order to demonstrate the quality of their research.

Writing ethnography

Ethnographers have struggled with the style of writing they should adopt, ranging from realist or authoritarian to confessional tales (Van Maanen 1988). After the textual turn, both fieldwork and writing has been riddled with tensions between experience and representation (Clifford and Marcus 1986). In the 1980s much of the ethnographic research has moved away from realist conventions towards experimentation with form and multiple authorial voices. Problems of description have become problems of representation.

Clifford and Marcus suggest ethnographic writing can be called fiction. They explore how ethnographic truths are partial, committed and incomplete. In the 1980s, self-reflexive writing developed, specifying the discourse of the informants as well as that of the ethnographer. A dialogical textual production emerged, locating cultural interpretation in many reciprocal contexts, so that culture became always relational. Clifford and Marcus privileged textual theory and textual form. Today the most extreme post-structural and post-textual claims have also been questioned (Morley 1997). Elsbeth Probyn has challenged reflexive ethnographers to consider what exactly they are reflecting on. She argues that reflexive writing privileges a type of 'self' that is not accessible to those who are written about. Many feminists, for example Leslie Roman (1993), have argued for materialism to be integrated into ethnographic writing.

Most of us in the research group have adopted ways of writing where the authorial 'I' is of particular concern when methodological issues are discussed (Gordon, Hynninen, Metso, Lahelma, Palmu and Tolonen 2000). Otherwise, our stories are not about ourselves in the field. We have integrated our own practices, reactions and emotions in our methodology. We have aimed to be as aware as possible about our own analysis and interpretation (Gordon, Holland and Lahelma 2000b). But our main focus in our respective writing ranges from practices, processes, cultures and texts to contexts. We have focused on ourselves in order to be reflexive, not in order to privilege our own selves over other selves. Our concern has been to be aware of the speaking 'I' or 'We'.

We write within the academy. Although we have all adopted a multi-disciplinary approach, each in our own way, combining elements from sociology, education, women's studies, feminist research and cultural studies, most of the researchers wrote in a disciplinary context. This is particularly pertinent to post-graduate students writing their theses. We had to, and wanted to, address audiences ranging from the academy to our own peers, and educational practitioners. Even when we write for disciplinary peers, they may have little experience or knowledge of ethnographic research (Wellin and Fine 2001).

The researcher should avoid harming participants (Murphy and Dingwall 2001). However, the experience of being written about can be startling. Despite anonymity, participants might recognize themselves, or recognize and misrecognize others. When Elina and I were interviewing the school students again in our transitions research, we gave them one article in the first follow-up interviews. In the subsequent follow-up interviews one young man explained to Elina that he had identified one of the young men quoted in the article, despite the use of a pseudonym. When Elina checked the article, she found that the young man mentioned had not been written about in the article at all. In a similar manner teachers thought they recognized their own school in the metaphor article, even though the analysis was based on metaphors collected in several schools besides the two research schools. However, when we reread the article, we found one reference to one of our research schools where we had explained the gendered composition of one particular class, and realized that the school was able to recognize itself from that discussion. This was inadvertent.

Otherwise our analysis concentrated on the secondary school as an institution in general, and the gist of the arguments did not pertain to particular schools.

On the other hand, sometimes participants do not recognize themselves when their discussion or actions have been placed in an analytical context. But there are numerous examples in ethnographic research where the participants do recognize themselves written about in a context that is unfamiliar to them and their talk or their practices may be interpreted in a way that disappoints them or gives them offence (Coffey 1999). However, we can never escape from the possibility that publication 'will cause private (or community) shame, even where it does not lead to public humiliation' (Murphy and Dingwall 2001: 341). Moreover, as Murphy and Dingwall suggest, the writer is not necessarily able to judge what will shame or harm participants.

Feminist writers in particular have suggested sharing interpretations with participants. This is not always possible. The participants may not have the time and inclination to read the researcher's texts. Or the participants may not be available to share the process as they may have moved on by the time the researcher has analysed data and started writing. Even when they are available, they may not be willing, for a range of reasons, to discuss interpretations. Rigoberta Menchu has suggested that anthropologists will never be able to understand different, alternative secrets (quoted in Yudice 1988: 230). Judith Stacey's ethnographic research on two women's extended networks involved intensive participation in the lives of the key informants. When Stacey wanted to share her texts with each of them, one informant suggested that she did not exactly recognize herself in the painful account of her life. But she suggested that Stacey nevertheless stick to what she had written, because as a researcher Stacey could never pin her down anyway (Stacey 1990).

Indeed Stacey (1988) has asked whether feminist ethnography is possible. We think it is. Whilst feminists cannot overcome or solve all questions of ethics, it is possible to be more or less sensitive to the research field and its participants. In Leslie Roman's (1993) research on punk-rock cultures, a shift to a more female-centred and collaborative perspective facilitated the young women's questioning of their position in this subculture. Moreover, in our collective project a feminist perspective has been important in our project group – even though there is no single 'feminist ethnography'. In terms of research practices it has helped us in our project group to develop collaborative research and be aware of its pitfalls. It has also helped us to deal with the inevitable tensions that close cooperation engenders and has encouraged us to develop collective analysis and writing, as well as writing carried out by individuals. As Beverley Skeggs suggests, 'just as there are multiple routes into ethnography, there are many different feminist ways through it' (2001: 428). Moreover, Skeggs argues that feminist ethnography has produced in-depth data about women's lives, and has challenged what is counted as knowledge.

Talking ethnography

When we address dissemination, written work is often privileged in the academic context. Researchers are posited as professionals who read and write. Data, whatever the methods of gathering, usually reaches the form of a written word, even when representations that are visual (or audio) are used as well. But researchers also talk, and ethnographers in particular talk a great deal whilst conducting research. When they are interacting with people in the field, most of the talk assumes a form of dissemination. Ethnographers' words are interpreted as clues about what they are interested in – 'informants' can either address those issues, side-step them or keep them hidden. As suggested above, ethnographers also talk about what they are doing and why when they negotiate entries into micro-situations in the field.

But ethnographers also talk in other professional contexts. They use their fieldwork in seminars, conferences and in their teaching. When I have introduced the concept of the abstract individual as a citizen in an introductory women's studies lecture, I have tried to illustrate this concept by citing girls and boys talking about themselves. This discussion draws on an analysis in our book (Gordon, Holland and Lahelma 2000). When I read what students write on the basis of the lectures, it is clear that these examples facilitate their understanding of socially differentiated possibilities of school students to occupy the position of a speaking 'I'.

But when young people's talk is cited, the audience often finds it amusing. The turn of phrase used may occasion laughter; their statements, extracted from the context of expression, may create mirth. There are situations where school students describe events with poignant, often intended irony. Their turn of phrase may demonstrate some of absurdities of everyday life at school, thus the laughter of the audience. Laughing makes me feel ambivalent sometimes, as I respect young people I have conducted research with. I am filled with gratitude when they pause to reflect on issues that I want to talk about with them. Even though I use a pseudonym, I know who the talking person is whose words are represented. And I need to engage in a mental leap – it is indeed a representation that I am representing – a double take, whereby no original authenticity is claimed or even sought for. In ethnographic research we have met and talked to people within social and material contexts as human actors, as thinking and feeling individuals. Yet when subjectivities of, and in, education are discussed, the focus is on shared constituents of those subjectivities, not on a specific individual's subjectivity – even when a particular person's talk is used to demonstrate that subjectivity (Gordon 1986: 250–1). Therefore, say, 'Ida', the pseudonym used to refer to a particular girl's talk, indeed is as constructed as the name she is given. When 'Ida's' voice is evoked in my writing, she is not representing herself – instead her words have been chosen by the researchers as a representation of the researchers' analysis, not as a representation of the living, talking girl whom I have encountered in interaction. Although ethnographic research aims to render accounts of everyday life, 'Ida' inhabits social and spatial relations in textual production (Gordon 1986: 250–1).

Another issue occasioned by talk is the question of what can and should be revealed. When I want to critically engage with educational politics and policies, I want to demonstrate that they do have impact, even though not directly, in everyday life at school. This means that fragments I use in this context usually do not demonstrate what might be called 'good practice'. I may illustrate how increasing pressures at school are manifested in situations where teachers are putting pressure on tired students who, for example, pause to lean against the wall or bang their heads on the desk, cry out in some irony that the amount of work they are expected to do amounts to torture, and that the time given to do it is insufficient, or moan that the lesson lasts too long. These vignettes give a very embodied, material sense of relentlessly coercive aspects of everyday life at school. Often they are lively enough to evoke forgotten painful experiences in listeners. Consequently the audience may interpret these episodes extremely negatively, laying the blame on individual teachers, for example. Again, this is not the intention. Social processes are more complex than that. Therefore, as we have discussed in the project group, we try to avoid using the most negative examples, and search for a similar extract in content, but less startling in style.

The collective context provided by the project helps us to make judgements about dissemination, although it is no guarantee that problems will not emerge, as the metaphor episode demonstrated. The episode had to be tackled by those of us who were interviewing teachers at the time. I was in that situation, and did not cherish it. Yet I was one of the co-authors of the initial article that occasioned the headlines in the national daily. The episode was even more keenly felt by a researcher who – although she had participated in the collective metaphor analysis – had not participated in the writing of the article. She was starting to interview teachers at that point, and an unexpected aspect of the interviews was an inevitable discussion of the newspaper article.

As, among professional researchers, writing and reading is more highly valued than talking and listening, issues of dissemination through talk have been particularly neglected. As ethnographers we want to render life into our accounts, whether spoken or written. Difficulties attached to this endeavour have been a collectively discussed concern in our project. Reaching ethically and politically appropriate solutions is nevertheless not an easy task.

Ongoing dissemination

The questions of dissemination have remained with us. The research group decided that we would write a more detailed, considered report aimed at non-academic people interested in education. The main issue we wanted to take up was difference in schools. We had several meetings discussing practices we had observed at school and planned a report aimed at teachers and educationalists. Our aim is to demonstrate the range of ways in which difference is produced in schools, whilst using examples of good practices we had observed (in relation to difference) and developing suggestions from these good practices. This work has been going on for a long time, as each of us researchers negotiates a difficult timetable.

We completed a draft and delivered it to Green Park and City Park, our research schools, with a certain amount of trepidation. On the basis of their comments we have finalized the report and it is to be published by the City of Helsinki Education Office (Lahelma and Gordon, forthcoming). Dissemination is therefore an ongoing concern for us and the story of our project continues. Elina and I have been doing transitions interviews with the school students we met (Gordon and Lahelma 2002). During the last interview round we gave them copies of our publications (if they wanted them). We are yet to hear what their reactions to these publications are, and at times we worry that they will hate them, that they will recognize or misrecognize themselves or each other, that they will not want to meet us again. . . . We shall interview them once more when they are about 22 years old. The ethics, politics and practices of writing about our work need to be addressed anew in each shifting context we talk or write in.

I suggested, in the title of this chapter, that dissemination involves many intricacies. 'Intricacy' refers to 'the state of being made up of many small parts or details' (*Collins Cobuild English Dictionary for Advanced Learners* 2002). Dissemination of ethnographic research on education is indeed entangled in educational politics and policies, research politics, professional collegial networks, academic evaluation, publication strategies and numerous human relationships with our colleagues, our employers, our research field and people there. We have gone into the field with our interests in citizenship, difference and marginalization. We had resolved to search for stories of cooperation, not just stories of conflict. At times our quest has left us bewildered, fraught or at the very least nervous. At times we have experienced joy and elation. At times, of course, it has been for us precisely what we have sought to capture in schools and in young people's trajectories: everyday life.

7 | Mis/representations: issues of control and closure in an academic career

Loraine Blaxter

Introduction

When I began work on this chapter I understood the study of dissemination to be about the movement of ideas. Dissemination of research, of ideas and experiences and ways of knowing, included writing and talk. It included communication with different audiences but it was also fundamental to a consideration of higher education careers, and to everyday practices of intellectuals, scholars and academics. The politics of dissemination concerned the contribution, or not, of ideas to emancipatory projects.

Only recently, since my work on dissemination began in 1997, have I paid attention, in writing of research, to my own presence in the field (Blaxter 2000). In consequence I have seen the ideas and activities that composed my life as 'the field' and dissemination as, also, about what ideas I, and others, take up and live within. This paper describes the making of this connection.

A 'professional' life story – research and writing

I have been preoccupied with how to live a life that enacted my values and beliefs while also earning a living. I have talked about experiences of trying to do this, with friends and colleagues involved in anti-racist, decolonizing, and women's movement actions. I have also used stories, of my own experiences and those of friends and colleagues, of ethical dilemmas and political contradictions, in teaching and in conversations around the kitchen table. Only some of this has been formally 'disseminated' – that is written for publication.

When I review what I have published, and what catches my interest for investigation and analysis, it is some external force or power that I sense is immanent in the field in which I am living and working. This interest becomes energy for writing for a public audience, even when the focus of research is firmly tied to a specific job of work, a project designed by my employers. The emotional impact of an incident or a phrase which might become the stuff of anecdotes, of talk, of day-to-day meaning-making has been also what provided the impetus for publication, when publication was a duty. I might prefer, or even be better at, conversation and dialogue but, for academic careers, talk and teaching is not enough. Because sometimes I fell silent alone, I have preferred to work and write collaboratively.

Writing for publication has, for me, been first and foremost about 'doing the job'. During the years (1980–90) when I was involved in community action and teaching outside the academy I did not write for publication. When I had to account for my activities, I saw community practice then as within Participatory Action Research, and so associated with social movements and adult education. I did not think to record this work. When I write for the job (in the 1970s as a 'good student' and then as a 'socially responsible' intellectual) this has been primarily stimulated by indignation at something I have heard or seen. I tried to make a context in which to criticize the ideas and actions of practitioners I met during fieldwork – agricultural extension officers, public health inspectors – and the policy they enact. I paid acute attention to words and phrases that were illustrative of naivety, or disrespect, for the complexity of other peoples' lives and a justification of the established order. I wrote in defence of a French peasant's sceptical view of economic development; in support of micro- and communal forms of businesses and critique of imposed laws.

Alongside 'doing the job' there were three other ideas about dissemination that did not have a name. However they travelled with me. These I associated with being socially responsible. This worried me during and after my PhD fieldwork and is described in this chapter. How to resolve the issue was elaborated specifically in my early career and while working in Papua New Guinea. First, all writing and talking had to be in accessible language. Secondly, that the priority audience for research was not the international academy, but students and practitioners. Thirdly, writing, like any other intellectual activity, tried to encourage, support, 'feed', critical (oppositional) social positions.

When I began working in Continuing Education in the 1990s this story changed. Writing, about how learning combined with other activities and responsibilities in adult lives, was in response to the main motifs of the literature. This was 'to ameliorate the dominant message of andragogical theory that the adult learner is an autonomous, self-directed and independent agent' (Hughes 2000: 286).

This chapter is different again. It began with memory and brings together two themes in research on academic careers and research dissemination. One was how to sustain my self-identity (as a good and responsible intellectual) in a University Continuing Education department in post-modern times. Two was my intense response to seeing, represented in a tourist guide, the people of my initial research site in the 1960s – the French Pyrenees. I examine the layers of ideas and coincidence uncovered by the label ('orientalist') I attached to what I saw written. An act of reading, and subsequently of memory, led me to consider the crisis of representation that has characterized qualitative research in general and in particular social anthropology. This theoretical angst had implications for my 'consciousness of life' (Pocock 1975: x) and sense of political connections and alliances. I turned to notice the separation I had maintained between my reading for pleasure (including reading books that were gifts), my personal family life and friendships and my scholarly life-storying.

The responsible student story

My professional self-identity has been attached to the idea of 'doing right' and 'being responsible'. The roots of this, which were about making research available and useful, are traced in this section. This self-identity, as 'a responsible student', was fundamentally challenged by a written representation of the people of the Pyrenees in a tourist guide. The section sets the research and dissemination context for that mis-representation.

The research process that produced my doctoral thesis (Blaxter 1971a) and my first publication (Blaxter 1971b) was conceptualized as fieldwork. I do not recall ever hearing of research as qualitative, for example, nor of research being disseminated. Looking back now, and considering changes in methodological discourses, it is probable that we never did use this terminology. I did however receive post-graduate research training in 1966–67 and I was preoccupied during the writing-up period 1969–71 with questions about the use of research, how to be relevant, what I could give back to the people with whom I had been close.

I was striving to be 'good' as a student and a researcher. Being 'good enough' as a researcher was, for me, about social responsibility. I had a personal desire to act in accordance with my ideals and values, and to judge myself positively. At the time, these concerns were private and personal – about me, my way of being a good person. I did not have this conceptualized as about social research ethics. Neither did I conceptualize any gender issues.

The PhD studentship brought with it a structure of expectations, which were communicated by the supervisor, and to which I submitted. I understood that I was to get a job as soon as the scholarship ran out, to write for publication and finish the dissertation in good time. This was to be done in order to secure the reputation of the whole post-graduate programme, and opportunities for future research students. My grant finished in the summer of 1969 and I took my field notes and my typewriter with me to take up a university teaching post (in Belfast) at the start of the new academic year. Two others, of this first cohort of PhD studentships, did the same.

In addition our supervisor produced two edited collections to which we were invited to contribute. I wrote for the first volume on 'Gifts and Poison' (Blaxter 1971b). This was focused on village economics and the politics of reputation and, indeed, marks a point of connection with the tourist guide entry. The second collection was on the diffusion of innovations.

It is possible now to trace the assumptions about relevance of research that infused the anthropology I read and is illustrated in those two edited volumes. We assumed, along with many others, that the subsistence rural way of life in Europe was vanishing (Mendras 1970; Franklin 1969; and subsequently Berger 1979). Anthropology was concerned with the interface between tradition and modernity. The research task was to find out and to describe how people of the little, local community were adapting to changes. How we did this was left up to each of us. What we were to write was detailed 'thick' descriptions with attention to interpersonal relations and local-level politics.

Conducting fieldwork 'in more or less isolated and "exotic" communities amounted to a kind of rite of passage by which the novice is transformed into the rounded anthropologist and invited into the ranks of the profession' (Epstein 1967: vii). By taking a job and 'entering the profession' I was doing the right thing by my supervisor, and by future students. Finishing the dissertation in good time was also important, although I felt, and thought I had remained, very marginal to 'the profession'.

How to do the right thing by the people with whom I had lived was another matter, and one that concerned me and my own idea of myself. While teaching and writing I began to feel ashamed that I did not have the skills to communicate in French outside the talk of the village. I did not know enough about agriculture, or European Union policy, to provide appropriate information to the farmers. I knew nothing about publishing. As a gesture, I produced an extra copy of the dissertation, which, through contact with a French sociologist, would be deposited in a research institute in France. That way I thought I had at least made an attempt to give something back in the direction of French scholarship.

Stories from the field

My initial fieldwork had a profound impact on my subsequent scholarship. Firstly different meanings of 'development', scepticism about the forms of progress being advocated by people with authority, attention to different, conflicting interests, became a key research theme. Initial fieldwork experience shaped my subsequent political and intellectual preoccupations most specifically with the articulation of modes of production and reproduction, and with class analysis. Conceptualizations of this have, of course, changed to include the technological and market changes associated with 'globalization'.

One story of this research which I have told, and which has been the main theme I have consciously disseminated, is different to that which I find written in the dissertation and the article. Indeed, until I looked again at what I had published, this (in Box 1) was what I remembered, and assumed I had written about. What I had recollected of my work was in the verbal accounts I gave of this fieldwork, which had been storied into my memory of what I had written. These are summarized in Box 1.

Carrying the field forward

This conversation, noted in Box 1, clearly had a deep impression on me. For example, in a research grant application in 1972, I wrote of the more general problem of the contact between rural communities and capitalist economic values. I also commented that the peasant who clings to his land is thought to be irrational, while at the same time, high-level civil servants consider it highly rational to invest in property in the country. Also the capitalization of agriculture versus tourism is related to conservationist issues.

I wanted my future research in Europe to be relevant to debates about international economic development and I wanted to speak out for rural

Box 1: Tale-telling as dissemination

This is a story of how wise and knowing the poorest people were. It is about how well the people of this area understood the social and economic forces that were impinging on them. It concerns the way in which 'nous paysans' understood that they were stereotyped as ignorant and foolish, and how they 'played' ignorant and foolish to get rid of people who, from their viewpoint, did not understand their interests.

For example, Paul told me that, when asked to sell land, he had refused by talking about how sentimentally attached he was to the family memories associated with the fields. Really, though, he told me, he knew that his land would be sold on to people with money to invest in building on it. Finally people would come from the towns to holiday houses and these people would think he was ignorant and foolish. His family didn't need more of that sort of person living locally.

He knew that money was of little value. You could not eat money. With land you could produce food.

---

resistance to conventional development trajectories. A European-wide network that aimed to link social research to policy had contacted me and I had undertaken some work with them. I had linked up with an oral history network in the UK as this felt like the direction that interested me for immediately useful research. But I did not feel that I could truly join the 'ranks of the profession' until I had worked in the Third World. Later that same year I moved to Papua New Guinea, with my partner, to undertake research for the office of the first elected Chief Minister of the government that would take the country from self-government to independence.

That period of my career, in Papua New Guinea, lay between my initial research in the French Pyrenees and the representation I saw published. During this period 'doing right' and 'being responsible' had attached to decolonization and anti-racism. I had worked on a 'decolonizing project' in research and teaching in Papua New Guinea. This project connected also to my personal life – my partner and children complete the 'other' section for race/ethnic group on the UK census form. I was emotionally attached by family relationships, through friendship, by reading and (occasionally) teaching with 'Third World scholarship'. On returning to the UK I had worked within a participatory action research ideal. This second aspect of my biography made the judgement 'orientalist' attached to research I had undertaken terribly compelling. It also contributed to the anxiety and shame that overcame me.

Publication – the uncertain audience

Looking at it now it seems the piece about my initial fieldwork which was written for publication (Blaxter 1971b) had an imagined audience which fits with the diffusionist research assumptions of the time. I wanted to shape my description to be relevant to development practitioners, specifically agricultural advisors. I wrote knowing that some anthropology was read in rural development sections of colleges – but having never met such students. In it I tried to draw conclusions about the potential for cooperation between farmers or commune-wide. This was an important 'development' theme at that time, indeed it was significant in the research I undertook subsequently.

For a quarter of a century I never thought about who might have read this. In 1988 a friend sent me a foolscap cyclostyled copy of the chapter, which she had found in a teaching resource store-box at the University of Zimbabwe. That was gratifying. It was troubling. What had it been used for? What meaning had been made? How had it got there? I remember this fifteen years later, thinking about dissemination and how ideas travel and are judged. This is to emphasize that I had all but forgotten what might have been disseminated through publication of my initial research.

Mis/re-presenting: the story of the tourist guide – an emotional response

This review of my initial research career, and recollection of dissemination of my initial fieldwork, was triggered by something I read. Or rather, how I remembered what I felt about something I read. The text, the feelings, and the anxiety and shame this surfaced are now considered. However, this is a learning journey that has just begun and is concerned with being a socially responsible intellectual in new times.

The mixed feelings I had had seeing 'my people' as 'the people of the Pyrenees' were etched in memory. I shall describe those contradictory feelings and sketch a commentary on this before moving on to consider in more detail what reflection on this mis-representation opened up. You might at any point now want to examine the text in Boxes 2 and 3.

Box 2: Travellers' tales

People of the Pyrenees
The people of the Pyrenees are of three nationalities. . . . They have always lived their lives as if frontiers did not exist . . .

Generally, the people of the Pyrenees are extremely friendly, although they tend to be formal, especially on the French side . . .

Depopulation . . . repopulation
The traditional life of the high mountains has changed drastically with the coming of mechanized agriculture on the plains. As mountain agriculture became less and less profitable, so younger people moved away to the towns. In much of the central Pyrenees in particular the population is only half what it was a century ago.

Village economics
The *old way of life*, though, is still apparent. The *custom* of **gifts** within the village, for example, has its *roots in the barter* system. If you live in a Pyrenean village for any length of time, and are accepted, then you will **receive presents of vegetables from neighbours and be expected to give something, produce or perhaps labour, in return**. . . .

Village life
Coupled with conservatism is a *parochialism* and introversion that extends right along both sides of the range. Only dire necessity has forced villages to cooperate . . .

Discover Pyrenees (1992: 50–51) Berlitz guide (found 19.2.01)

Box 3: A travel guide entry remembered – reconstituted from memory

---

The peasants are proud and fiercely protective of their reputation for independence but not socially isolated. There are co-operative relationships between households which exchange land use, labour assistance, tools and food. There is also the potential for getting help from neighbours in emergency. They are rich in social connections but also reluctant to ask for help unless they can negotiate a return of service. History has left the people of the 'empty quarter' wary of social obligations.

(written 9.1.01)

- First, I was delighted because there (Box 2), in print, was an account of (the village) that fitted with my own understanding. What I discovered was valid and reliable.
- Secondly, before this response was finished, I was suspicious. Where did this come from? It could be of course that they have read my work and summarized it here. It was not referenced.
- Thirdly, another feeling, this time of horror. This has made these people exotic, the stuff of 'travellers' tales' – it is orientalist.
- And then I felt terribly responsible. If I was the (delighted) researcher then I made this possible, even though I've always tried so hard to 'do right'.

In these responses which, as I said, were powerfully etched in my memory were several themes. There was the **desire** to have research verified and an interest in **citations**. Here was an acknowledgement of the researcher's **power** and so **responsibility**. And alongside it recognition of the **risk** of exposing yourself to judgement. For me also here was shame – I saw myself as implicated in a hegemonic discourse, in 'orientalism'.

Writing from memory – a note about method

As I began to reflect on these responses to recognition, re-appropriated and re-presented, and to write I encountered a feeling of ignorance. I was not explicitly intellectually engaged with more than a fragment of post-colonial or post-structuralist research literatures. Because I knew about the fragments, I felt ignorant. Additionally, as I reflected and indeed wrote, I discovered that my 'reading for pleasure' had entered my consciousness. This meant that I was thinking within a discourse that I partially recognized. And, as I thought about myself and orientalism, this was infused with what seemed like coincidence – but was not. I entered the muddle of chaos/complexity! I made a pragmatic decision to write within the discourses that were present on my bookshelves. As this work progressed I recognized that these books also marked social connections – to friends, partner, children, colleagues past and present.

Memory or dream?

But before I got to that understanding, the 'muddle' and chaos intensified. The anxious turn to reconsider my own research career had been triggered by something I read. I needed to relocate the text that I had seen in a travel guide. I remembered, clearly, that the text was in an illustrative box. I decided to use a copy of the box from the book and to examine it in more detail. There were two guides to the Pyrenees on bookshelves, both purchased when I returned to the village in 1992. The pages on the department of Ariege, where I had worked, were well thumbed. I could not find any text that resembled what I had seen. In one the name of the village in which I had lived did occur – in a box about bear trainers. But nothing about gift giving.

Frustrated, and a little troubled, I took a break. Then I went back, searched again, still drew a blank and so turned to some other work. A week later I tried again and still could not find what I was looking for. This time I went to the library and bookshop in town, and looked at all the tourist and travel guides to France. I got all caught up in this. When I could not find the text I also could not remember which guide I had looked in before, or whether I had looked in the same edition.

When I could not find the empirical evidence for what I had seen, I thought I must have dreamt it. Indeed I began to wonder if there was a literature on dreams and educational research: I found, on my bookshelves 'dreaming, with all it implies of discontinuity and displacement' (Aiken 1989: 115). That sounded right! The feeling that this text was real was so strong that I went out for the evidence again. Twice in distress in a bookshop I bought a popular, heavily promoted book and went home to a corner of a sofa to read and lose the day. This was becoming a psychological drama.

Finally I decided that I would go ahead with planning this chapter, and reflecting on this experience of research representation, knowing that it was probably a dream and the emotional response said something about dissemination, and about how we take up ideas unconsciously. Over a vacation I told my son what I was working on, and how odd it had become. And he said: 'That wasn't a dream. You told me about finding the example in a book and being pleased and then shocked.' We could not remember when this was. Last year or years ago? He, while sure it was not a dream, saw that, dream or not, this was still interesting. So, of course, I kept going to look for the material evidence as if the wisdom of this dream is not enough. I wrote a version of the content of the Box 3 as I recalled it.

In the next section I comment on these texts before turning to consider the 'crisis of representation' and the 'professional anxiety' associated with the 'orientalist' label. At this point I invite you to read, if you have not done so already, the content of the boxes. In Box 3 I try to recreate what I thought I had dreamt that I read. Box 2 gives an extract from the text that, because I did not give up searching, I eventually discovered.

Different representations – an analytic response

In comparing these texts (Boxes 1, 2, 3), I can see why I might have associated Box 2 with the village I had lived in, although it was about the people of the whole region. This was because:

- I had published in a book about gifts, and 'gifts' were mentioned under heading of 'village economics'.
- I can see what it was that thrilled me. Here was an account of village economics that included the giving of gifts, which I had selected to write about.
- I can also see what shocked me. The authors have used elements of the vocabulary that created 'under-development' – tradition, custom, barter, parochialism, an 'old' way of life.

I had responded from within the realm of jokes about 'the anthropologist'. Thus:

- I had read about 'my people' and yet they wrote of the people of the whole Pyrenean region. I (Box 3) wrote of the peasants of one village in one valley.
- In trying to recapture what I had read I wrote of 'the people of the Pyrenees' as 'peasants'. It was an important theoretical concept that has negative connotations in everyday English. The Augustois described themselves as '*nous paysans*', but how that word is understood depends upon the listener (see Berger 1979 and below).
- I wrote of economic and political relations using terse and technical words: exchange, negotiate, return, service. I write 'about' the people. I did not include my experience of living in the village in the summary.
- We can see also that the guide takes a more personal tone in addressing the reader: 'If you live in a Pyrenean village . . . then you will receive presents.' This preyed on my mind. Did the guide seem to suggest that in giving presents these people were strange? What they had written was what anyone might discover through living in a village for a length of time. I did not and had not seen exchanging gifts as peculiar to these

villages, but rather as quite common human social practice. I had given and received gifts, of fruit, vegetables and food, wherever else I had lived, in Brighton, Belfast, Port Moresby and Leamington Spa. Was that because my extended-family culture constructed the community I inhabited? Or was it because my 'consciousness of life' created what I saw as social? Or because gift giving is not an 'old way of life'?

• My immediate response, and this reflection, also revealed a 'gender-free zone'. Neither the guide, nor my reconstruction, say anything about the gender of gift giving (yet see Blaxter and Hughes 2000) or associate gifts with domestic and subsistence production, with 'women's work'.

Why had I seen this, in an instant, as orientalism? How far can this label be attributed to the mode of writing, and how far to the emotional sensitivities of the reader. It is this I explore next, although I am conscious that these texts invite your re-interpretation.

Representation and responses

I have already described my immediate emotional responses to reading, and having to write, this. In this section of the paper I want to indicate where these responses to being re-presented have taken me and say something about my method.

Initially I reviewed my academic career with a focus on research and dissemination in four periods. One was the initial fieldwork in the French Pyrenees and the ideas about research and dissemination with which I associated it (1967–72). This review was the basis of the 'responsible' student story in this paper. Secondly was teaching and research as part of what I had thought of as a 'decolonizing project' in Papua New Guinea (1973–78). Thirdly was the period of ten years in the UK combining temporary or part-time employment with community action within an ideal of participatory action research. Finally was a period of secondment to an action learning partnership. In this initial review I put off examining my employment within a University Continuing Education Department and I concentrated on professional aspects of my self-identity.

In this review I focused on the ideas that travelled with me to locate my emotional response to the travel guide text (Box 2), and the inevitability and value of the label 'orientalist.' I felt troubled by relying entirely on my own memory and my stories of the past, but to gather documents to supplement my memory of all of these was going to take time. So I trawled my files and bookshelves.

I decided, pragmatically, to rely upon the books that surrounded me, checking their dates, as an indication of the ideas that were gathered around me. I looked for evidence to confirm that I had read them – notes in the margins, phrases underlined, pages turned down. I noticed that some I had bought, some were gifts. Many of these books, including those that mention orientalism, to which I turned only became associated with scholarly activity in this attempt to reflect on dissemination. This pragmatic choice of method showed me the association of ideas with my social network. That dissemination is part of the everyday.

Orientalism as a discourse

Orientalism (the term I attached to the text in Box 2) is a discourse associated with colonization, the concept originates in literary criticism with Edward Said (1978). Said showed how, in writing about other people, Western scholars and novelists have created an orientalist discourse. Through the orientalist discourse the West has been enabled to 'recognise itself by defining itself against the East' (Wisker 2000: 17). The scholarly construction of orientalism is supported by corporate institutions which 'make statements about it, authorising views of it, describing it, by teaching about it, settling it, ruling over it' (Said 1978: 3).

Adopting this label, I had associated my initial fieldwork with 'traveller's tales', with colonialism, and how research is harnessed to power. The label 'orientalism' had resurfaced the very issues that had troubled me within anthropology, and also brought close to me 'discourse' – a concept I used but a theoretical position I had not engaged with.

Methodology and colonialism

Several dimensions of anxiety can be associated with anthropological research. These have been seen as historical, methodological, theoretical and ethical. Each of these can be associated with 'orientalism' and with 'dissemination'.

Anthropology and colonialism
Anthropologists have been associated with colonialism. Colonialism controlled and silenced, subordinated and separated people within hierarchies. Anthropology is held particularly responsible for the production of the 'travellers' tales' with which the West created what Edward Said named as an orientalist discourse. This label then, neatly opened me to consider the angst associated with this profession, and my uneasy separation from it.

Methodological angst
One aspect of continuous methodological debate, in anthropology as in other fields of practice, is 'on the science side' (Geertz 2000: 94–5). We

might have rejected binary paradigms, and yet anthropological careers (like those of feminist scholars in the academy) were caught up by paradigm wars. Some self-questioning has persisted because of the power of the science rationalist discourse. This, again as Geertz says of the USA, dominates 'the funding sources, the professional organizations, journals and research institutions', and is 'nicely pre-adapted to the bottom-line mentality' (2000: 95).

Theoretical doubt
Another aspect of doubt is less about whether 'research is rigorous than about whether it is decent' (Geertz 2000: 95). This moral doubt becomes an anxiety about the representation of the Other. The question of the moral 'decency' of research away from home is linked to dissemination by Smith (1999), who comments that: 'Travellers' tales had wide coverage. Their dissemination occurred through the popular press, from the pulpit, in travel brochures . . . and in oral discourse' (L. Smith 1999: 2, 9).

Fieldwork ethics
A further area of doubt concerns the political and ethical dimensions of fieldwork. These were not discussed in my preparation for fieldwork. Using Geertz (2003: 37) again, 'the imbalance between the ability to uncover problems and the power to solve them, and the inherent moral tensions between investigator and subject' has worried me since.

Participatory action research (PAR) and research alliances

From the early 1970s there were three moves to reduce these problems: through writing the self in, sometimes autobiographically; by researching 'up' the social hierarchy; and by combining research with action, as in participatory action research. The second two I had embraced. They were all three features of feminist research. 'Researching up' included providing information which might contribute to struggles against power-holders to transform powerful institutions (as with the Equal Opportunities research in the UK of the early 1980s). Research of this kind was disseminated, usually at the end of the research process, to trade unions and social movements directly, as well as through more scholarly routes. My period of research on laws in Papua New Guinea had been in this mould.

Researching up and participatory action research (PAR) had problems with respect to funding unless they fitted closely with public policy. This was particularly the case in participatory action research, where ideally the 'problem' to be investigated was not to be named by the researcher or the funder but by the research participants, together. This required either a specialist agency to connect people or organizations with research needs and researchers (like some university 'science shops' or outreach research centres), or the researcher needed to participate in community organizations.

I was particularly attracted to the PAR research model, which had been developed in and through practice in marginalized communities. It involved the researcher working in partnership with people; combining education with research, and research with critique. It engaged actively, it seemed to me, with problems of being useful and relevant and of giving back and challenging power, and it was being developed by people to whom I felt ideologically connected. Within social anthropology some researchers had used it to help villagers wrest some control of 'rural development' (Huizer and Mannheim 1979). In decolonization there was the practice, reported by Mbilinyi (1982) and Mies (1983), that linked closely to adult education and movements by and for women.

These practices were also present in the women's movement in 'the north' through, for example, the accounts of Maria Mies (1983) and Patricia Maguire (1987), both of whom worked with women in refuge from violence. Patricia Maguire worked explicitly within an adult education context. For myself, without an attachment to a university, and without the discipline of having to write for the job, the project, practices and discoveries from an exploration of the action research model went unrecorded. Indeed that was the case of most of the work undertaken in old town Leamington through two 'collectives', Bath Place Community Venture and the independent 'Other Branch' bookshop. Significantly, workers or volunteers, who were also post-graduate research students, produced publications about praxis in the community project (Brown 1992; Shotten 1993).

Who speaks and who listens?

The label orientalist had opened to me consideration of where methodological angst associated with research and 'right practice' had placed me. It opened for me an exploration of the ways in which discourse(s) 'controls, silences or enables the expression of knowledge' (Wisker 2000: 17). 'Orientalism' enabled. I did not like the label. But it compelled a re-view and exploration. It opened me to a problem that had lost a name. 'Names limit but enable discourse' and 'without maps and labels . . . we could not speak' (Wisker 2000: 79).

The label, for me, reinserted 'representational anxiety' in the politics of research and so the politics of dissemination. It also uncovered the extent to which I had 'listened in' through general reading to feminists, many in the academy, while seeing myself as marginal, an intellectual on the outside. The word helped me recognize the conversations I had overheard through reading, and the strength of my desire to be connected to subaltern scholarship.

In this final section I reconsider and represent connections between my research career and Edward Said's writing. I move through coincidence to locate myself in relationship with friends and family who share experiences of otherness, exile and migration.

A story of social connection

In the years I had worked outside the academy, I had sustained connections to certain writers and themes and to people who shared these interests. So connection to ideas is represented in my family and friends. My two sons carry names from African researcher-activists. I have been listening in on conversations between 'Third World' activists and scholars and women fighting multiple colonialisms. We, my social network, have bought and read essays and fiction about struggle and (particularly, in my case) about exile, migration, refuge, travel and survival on the margins. We have given these texts as gifts. This writing travelled well. We found 'common likeness' in common differences.

Within this setting, Edward Said's term 'orientalism' was a compelling label to give myself. Two of his books were at home. I gave *Orientalism* (1978) as a gift to my partner. *After the Last Sky* (1986) by Said with the photographer Jean Mohr was a gift from a friend to us both. Jean Mohr had collaborated with John Berger in representing in words and photos the life of a country doctor and of migrants in European cities. Berger's book on the French peasants, *Pig Earth* (1979), had been a gift to me.

John Berger (1979), working from France, wrote of 'peasants'. He sees them as the great survivors through diverse forms of resistance to the state and markets and the judgement of elites. Working within a more literary tradition, he did not have a methodological problem of observation and representation. His project was 'to capture a way of life which is passing' in both fiction and essay. *Pig Earth* is a work of fiction in which 'everyday gossip, the tales, the events long past or present are narrated in a voice which is the peasants' own'. His portrayal of Lucie Cabrol was then reworked and became compelling *Theatre de Complicite*. Friends introduced us to this theatre.

From this literary standpoint there is no shame about representing the other. Because what Berger is representing is the human condition in a way that invites an emotional response which is political. And labelling the human condition is, of course, political. The question is always about who speaks and who is listening. How to speak to the 'otherness' in one another, the common likeness of feeling exiled, excluded and silenced, and to begin to dismantle rigid barriers, while also recognizing where any one of us may have the luxury of being able to pass across borders. There does not even seem to be embarrassment about ignoring gender in 'the' human condition.

By turning my attention back towards the post-colonial writers on my bookshelves I re-covered, now more self-consciously, Spivak and Gunew's understanding of the urge to 'rage against the history that has written an abject script' (Spivak and Gunew 1989: 416) into which we may feel inserted by certain discourses, and which may sometimes silence. I want to borrow from Spivak and Gunew the following quotation because it was produced in a discussion about the problem of mis-representations:

> It is not a solution, the idea of the disenfranchised speaking for themselves, or the radical critics speaking for them: this question of representation, self-representation, representing others, is a problem. On the other hand we cannot put it under the carpet with demands for authentic voices; we have to remind ourselves that, as we do this, we might also be compounding the problem even as we try to solve it.
>
> (Spivak and Gunew 1989: 417)

Thus:

> For me the question 'who should speak?' is less crucial than 'who will listen?' . . . There are many subject positions which one must inhabit, one is not just one thing. This is when political consciousness comes in . . .
>
> (Spivak and Gunew 1989: 413)

I concluded that the texts on my shelves were no coincidence. This was neither a 'wind-born process' of diffusion (Rudduck 1973) nor a systematic and planned dissemination. I had been listening to certain voices because they resonated with my political consciousness and some subject positions. They spoke to exile, and to movement, and to marginality and to alliances. But, in speaking to my feelings of alienation, they also spoke to an old angst about colonial anthropology, and about not having all the skills necessary for collaborative action. They also reminded me that ethical dilemmas in research and scholarship need not only be solved by proximate partnerships or by adult education. Politically sensitive intellectuals, without research funding, and without regular employment, are politically active through writing. And through writing we may save one anothers' lives. This is when political consciousness comes in.

A conclusion?

In the work out of which this paper developed I have come to recognize the layered ways in which research becomes 'a project of the self' and, in this case, revealed the 'no woman's land', and the internal barriers and silences, that are aspects of my autobiography (Acker 1981). If I had known at the beginning that the investigation of 'dissemination' would take such a turn I might not have begun. Working on this, alone, it was almost impossible to move towards an 'act of political accusation and engagement, rather than the confessional mea culpa' (Walsh 2001).

This, it seems to me, is a tantalizing question about what we read and what we are attending to, consciously and unconsciously. On my own bookshelves, well thumbed some of them, was a rich collection of novels, memoirs, diaries, autobiographies stretching from 1960 to the present. I had collected the testimonies of oppressed groups and women writing about their own, diverse, lives. I had a rich collection on the ideologies of developing nations, critiques of colonialism from within, the voices of the damned, and writings by men and women exploring and challenging racial identities.

From within my teaching in social anthropology and sociology of race relations and under-development, there were piles of photocopies associated with the politics and ethics of imperialist research and the debate between scholars and activists in social movements and community development. What I had not done was engage with how these ideas and these debates had shaped my sense of myself, personally or emotionally, and not only been the context in which I acted. I remembered, with a clarity and (sometimes guilty) rage, scenes and encounters in which I had felt labelled, silenced, written-out, 'othered'. I had closed my mind to these direct experiences. Indeed, some I had stored/closed away behind rehearsed other stories.

What the label 'orientalist' helped me do was to rediscover the value of personal testimony and biography as a work for myself. It also enabled me to see how writing and reading have the potential to contribute, below consciousness, to the formation or maintenance of political consciousness.

The idea of writing 'for yourself' is well rehearsed in feminist writing. There is also an understanding that 'writing to save your own life' might, at the same time, be writing with social purpose, raising consciousness and building solidarity. Thus telling secret knowledge might connect the dispersed, dispossessed and fragmented 'Daughters of Copperwomen' (Cameron 1983). Using my bookshelves to revision my research career forged a reconnection to my social networks. However, from within this story it became hard, alone, to make theoretical links. To achieve this ending, dialogue is needed.

Opening a political dialogue

How do we connect this reflection on my life story back to gender and practices of politics and disseminating research? After a long dialogue with Abdulhusein Paliwala I draw four themes from the story told in this paper. You may, of course, make other meanings.

1 *Disseminator subject and Disseminated object.* We as researchers tend to think of dissemination as our responsibility and (rightly) problematize our, and others', roles in the (mis)representation of research. And yet, we are also subjected to dissemination and therefore part of the chain, circle or chaos of dissemination. The story of the tourist guide, especially the dream, is a dramatic realization of the collision between the two – of the disseminator being subjected to her own dissemination, returning as a distorted Chinese whisper.

2 *Commodification.* The story is also of the commodification of research. Through effects best described as chaos/complexity the research becomes (mis)represented and orientalized in the market place of tourism. The subjects of the research, the people of Auguste, had no benefit from the research except perhaps from personal engagement with the researcher when she was there. Perhaps post-research dissemination activity contributed (but there are no peasants left to benefit) to a current realization that peasant perceptions are not ignorant and that peasants had a very good notion of development issues.

3 *The implications of a fractured career.* This is a life storied from a self-perception of a marginalized academic. The marginalization has been sustained in part as a result of life decisions which have a gendered basis – the abandonment of the notion of a settled academic career to accompany a partner, to live and work in Papua New Guinea. Becoming cut off from the labour market at the birth of a second child (which, in this life history, coincided with the Thatcher period). Becoming flexible labour and undertaking a variety of academic and community-based work, some paid, some unpaid. And this flexibility increased marginalization through lost access to a university library. This gender-fractured career had multiple effects. On the one hand, it reinforced a lack of power in the market place for participatory styles of knowledge production and use, with the consequence of making the task of engagement with a fully paid-up malestream academic culture a difficult one. On the other, it contributed to the very connectivities that enabled Said, Berger, Mies, Mbilinyi, Spivak, etc. to jostle together on the shelves and in the mind. This could enable the creation of a gendered 'subaltern' otherness, to a transgressive dissemination which linked conversations round the table with friends, women's groups and issues, community concerns, academic existence (however marginalized). And in such milieux we may learn from, and communicate with, students and colleagues.

4 Castell's (see Hoskyns 2000) work on networking has dominated recent thinking on the subject of political connections and metaphors for forms of social interaction. Putnam's work on social capital (see Blaxter and Hughes 2000) has become part of mainstream thinking on 'community'. Putnam's work silences gendered work. Castell's network metaphor in relation to gender provides space for gender networks. Neither

relates sufficiently to the specific impact of women who transgress the public/private frontiers of academic, community and home networks. This very marginalization and fractured existence may make these women's individual impact limited in each field. Yet, their transgressive strength in numbers contributes to the interconnectedness and survival of feminist and subaltern discourses and struggles. There is potentially much affinity between this story and the idea of 'transversal politics' or 'rooting and shifting' which Catherine Hoskyns describes as the new politics, in which people who are 'rooted' in particular membership and identities 'shift' to a situation of communication with those in different circumstances.

However, there is (an)other reality in plenty of shifting. . . . And can we all 'root'?

8 | Dissemination, or critique and transformation?

Bronwyn Davies

Disseminate: To distribute or scatter about, diffuse. [C17: from Latin disseminare, from DIS- + seminare, to sow, from semen seed]
(Collins English Dictionary, 1979)

The word *disseminate* derives from semen – the fluid containing spermatozoa that is ejaculated from the male genital tract. 'Seminal' also derives from semen, though the familiar meaning of 'highly original and important' also keeps company with 'rudimentary or unformed' (Collins English Dictionary, 1979). In this paper I want to work beyond the semiotic sub-text of 'dissemination' in which academic work is male, and is derived from male ideas – men scattering their seed to form into something separate from them. I do not want to entirely abandon the element of scattering, but to work with it and beyond it to 'gestation' and 'birth', to transformation and responsibility.

Deleuze's idea of the text as rhizomatic begins with scattering, but a scattering that potentially moves to create something new – new alignments that shake things up. Deleuzian texts can be:

> read, used, as modes of effectivity and action which, at their best, scatter thoughts and images into different linkages or new alignments without necessarily destroying their materiality.... Instead of the eternal status of truth, or the more provisional status of knowledge, texts have short-term effects, though they may continue to be read for generations. They only remain effective and alive if they have effects, produce realignments, shake things up. In Deleuzian terms, such a text, such thought, could be described as fundamentally moving, 'nomadological' or 'rhizomatic.'
>
> (Grosz 1995: 126–7)

In this textual move Deleuze opens a space in which the idea of selves as over-determined (both as writers and as readers) is replaced with readers who bring text to life.

Barthes, too, focuses on the importance of the reader, who *plays* texts in the way a musician plays a score. A musician brings the music to life, bringing an embodied reading of the score to life in the playing of it. In relation to written texts, Barthes recommends that we

> attempt to abolish (or at least diminish) the distance between writing and reading, not by intensifying the reader's projection into the work, but by linking the two together, into one and the same signifying practice . . . [The reader] *plays* the Text . . . The Text . . . solicits from the reader a practical collaboration. . . . [T]o be bored [by a text] means one cannot produce the text, play it, release it, *make it go.*
>
> (Barthes 1986: 62–3)

In addition to shifting the act of meaning-making towards the reader, Foucault realigns author and text. He suggests we will come to a time when the author is no longer seen as the source of meaning. Instead we will look at texts to see what they are capable of discursively producing:

> I think that, as our society changes, at the very moment when it is in the process of changing, the author function will disappear, and in such a manner that fiction and its polysemous texts will once again function according to another mode, but still with a system of constraint – one that will no longer be the author but will have to be determined or, perhaps, experienced [*expérimenter*].
>
> . . . We would no longer hear the questions that have been rehashed for so long: Who really spoke? Is it really he and not someone else? With what authenticity or originality? And what part of his deepest self did he express in his discourse? Instead there would be other questions, like these: What are the modes of existence of this discourse? Where has it been used, how can it circulate, and who can appropriate it for himself? What are the places in it where there is room for possible subjects? Who can assume these various subject functions? And behind all these questions, we would hear hardly anything but the stirring of an indifference: What difference does it make who is speaking?
>
> (Foucault 1998: 222)

This should not be read as the abandonment of the author and his or her responsibility in the writing. Rather it is a movement away from the tendency to interpret the meaning of texts according to what we take ourselves to know about a particular author's personal life history, with attendant presuppositions about intentions and emotions and even unconscious motivations. What is of interest to Foucault is the text itself and what it is capable of. In this, like Barthes, he moves responsibility, in part, away from the author and on to the reader. He says of his own writing:

> I have no way of knowing how people interpret the work that I have done. It is always a great surprise to me that my works have been translated abroad and even that my works are read in France. To speak frankly, I hope that my work interests ten or a hundred people; and, if it is a question of a larger number, I am always a bit surprised. From my point of view, it's that my name, Foucault, is easy to pronounce in Japanese; for example, much easier than Heidegger. That is a joke of course. I believe that somebody who writes has not got the right to demand to be understood as he had wished to be when he was writing; that is to say from the moment when he writes he is no longer the owner of what he says, except in a legal sense. Obviously, if someone criticises you and says that you're wrong, interpreting badly your arguments, you can emphasise what you wanted to express. But, apart from that case, I believe that the freedom of the reader must be absolutely respected. A discourse is a reality which can be transformed infinitely. Thus, he who writes has not the right to give orders as to the use of his writings.
>
> (Foucault in interview in Carette 1978: 111)

Barthes, too, wishes a movement beyond the fascination (even obsession) with the author as one whose personal thoughts and feelings are the 'lyrical' source and reason for writing. He insists, rather, that we understand both self and writing to be coincidental and to emanate from a plenitude in which text/writer remain flexible and open to new meanings:

> . . . the writer today, it seems to me, can no longer be content to express his own present according to a lyrical project: he must learn to distinguish the speaker's present, which remains grounded in psychological plenitude, from the present of the locution, which is as flexible as that locution and in which event and writing are absolutely coincidental.
>
> (Barthes 1986: 15)

Conception and gestation and birth

When I think of conception and gestation in relation to writing, these metaphors suggest something internal to the body, inward-looking, solitary. While this is an essential part of what writing is, I also want to extend the metaphor I'm playing with here, to make clear that it is also deeply interactive and discursive. In my woman's body the child is conceived when the sperm is taken in by the sticky filaments on the outside of my ova. The child unfolds its life in a fold in my body. It is of me (but not only of me) and is, unquestionably, becoming a being that has its own life – a life that is never independent of the discursive constructions of it. Just so, when I write, I am drawing on the discursive possibilities opened up for me in the words of others; I am reaching into and reading them as they take life on and through the folds of my own body.

> FOLDING
> The folds in the earth's surface
> the hills and valleys of my childhood—
> ancient eruptions and erosions.
>
> The curve of a wave
> lifting itself above me, fills with light
> swirls over and around me, and is gone.
>
> The fold of arms holding
> a small child's body—
> each the other's landscape.
>
> With/in the intricate involuted folds
> of my internal/external body—
> words and images take root.
>
> Writing, I trace these folds
> I touch them intimately—
> and unfold.
>
> Unfold
> in laughter, in jouissance, or rage—
> or slowly, like the petals of a chrysanthemum.
> (Davies 2000: 62)

As the words unfold onto the page I am also imagining the audience to whom I am speaking; I am constructing through the words on the page the reader who can enter into the ideas that are unfolding there. I want the words I have written to become playable in particular ways, both by me and by people other than me. So I draft and redraft until the thing I want to say is lucidly there, able to be picked up and read – even drawing others to it, to pick it up and read it. So the text becomes a meeting point, a collaboration, a possibility of movement on to something else, both for me and for the reader.

There is a danger in this metaphor that it draws me towards an investment of too much power and responsibility in the child/reader. I write only what the reader can hear/play. I stand back to let the reader/child make his or her own way with the text. There is a certain conception of motherhood that would encourage such a reading. But I do not want either myself (or the reader of this text) to fall into that binary trap. The text/mother is life-giving.

It opens the possibility of life in different forms. It lets go too, as part of the same act. In the final movement of this chapter then, I want to turn to the transformative power of text and to the author's responsibility in relation to the texts s/he writes.

Transformation and responsibility

Those who resist poststructuralist writing sometimes argue that it can only produce critique and that it is incapable of transformative action. Foucault's answer to this is:

> ...I don't think that criticism can be set against transformation, 'ideal' criticism against 'real' transformation.
>
> A critique does not consist in saying that things aren't good the way they are. It consists in seeing what type of assumptions, of familiar notions, of established, unexamined ways of thinking the accepted practices are based.
>
> ... There is always a little thought occurring even in the most stupid institutions; there is always thought even in silent habits.
>
> Criticism consists in uncovering that thought and trying to change it; showing that things are not as obvious as people believe, making it so that what is taken for granted is no longer taken for granted. To do criticism is to make harder those acts which are now too easy.
>
> Understood in these terms, criticism (and radical criticism) is utterly indispensable for any transformation.
>
> ... as soon as people begin to have trouble thinking things the way they have been thought, transformation becomes at the same time very urgent, very difficult, and entirely possible.
>
> (Foucault 2000a: 456–7)

In finding ways to see the world against the grain of dominant discourses, in making those discourses and their constitutive work visible, the writer's task is to loosen the grip of realities whose inevitability had previously been unquestionable.

When we choose those discourses on which we want to cast our deconstructive analytic gaze, we do not do so randomly, separate from the life that is going on around us. Our gaze inevitably falls on aspects of our own life or on the lives of those around us. We find a problem, and we do so alongside others who are also already finding the same problem. We come to see a problem – such as unnecessary violence, or a problem of profound neglect – and we see it, not as a unique and random occurrence, but as produced out of available discourses and practices. Those discourses and practices have a logic that appears to those who take them up to be ineluctable – until we begin our critical, deconstructive work. Our work arises both out of our own location in the world and in discourse, and out of the collective struggles in which we are caught up.

Foucault points out that his theoretical work is always in some sense a fragment of his own autobiography as he experiences it in relation to life unfolding around him:

> Every time I have tried to do a piece of theoretical work it has been on the basis of elements of my own experience: always in connection with processes I saw unfolding around me. It was always because I thought I identified cracks, silent tremors, and dysfunctions in things I saw, institutions I was dealing with, or my relations with others, that I set out to do a piece of work, and each time was partly a fragment of autobiography.
>
> (Foucault 2000a: 458)

Like Foucault, I conceive of writing as both autobiographical and as an intensely collective act, connected to the processes I see unfolding around me. The conventions of writing may lead us to construe what we write as having sprung somehow out of our own heads, or out of our fingers on the keyboard. But when we write we are already deeply implicated in multiple layers of conversation with others – authors, editors, friends and colleagues, family, the media – out of which spring the possibility of the question we want to ask and the possible ways of answering it. At the same time, writing is intensely personal. It does not rise out of the discursive contexts that are somehow separate from our embodied selves, our inmost passions and desires. For me, writing springs from a reading of the depth-surfaces of my own body. Like Cixous (in Cixous and Calle-Gruber 1997: 29), who talks about 'the pearls and corals of the "language" of the soul', I am interested in these jewels that are experienced as deeply private and personal, but that are also keys to collective knowledges. These are not just keys lying randomly to be picked up, or ignored, but keys which are in some sense 'overdetermined', demanding to be picked up and used to unfurl a collective wisdom.

I invited my readers in *(In)scribing Body/Landscape Relations* to interact with what I wrote, not solely at the level of *logos*, or intellect, but as embodied readers, with feelings, with imagination, with the capacity to know differently, with the capacity to read from the body. I adopted a style of writing that is poetic, an invitation rather than an instruction, to know bodies, and to know them with/in multiple folds in physical, political, and discursive landscapes. What I invite the reader to 'know' as a result of their reading is as much in the manner of what I have written as it is in the content. It is in the manner of writing that I have attempted to give meaning differently, to open a space for other possibilities of understanding. What I am in that writing is the text, I am the flexible possibilities that the text opens up.

(In)scribing Body/Landscape is not just about finding keys to unlock

cultural meanings of bodies and landscapes in order to make them visible. It is also about transgression, about finding other ways to speak and write with the grain of bodies and landscapes. It is an exploration of the power of language, not only as it seeps into bodies and shapes the very grain of them, but also as a powerful force that individuals and collectives can use to retell lives against the grain of what Morrison (1993) calls 'dead language'. Through dead language, Cixous suggests, we become ignorant of ourselves and have no agency. We are like corks, bobbing about on the sea of discourse:

> The most incredible is to notice to what extent we are all ignorant of ourselves. To what extent we are 'stupid', that is to say without imagination. To what extent we are sort of corks without poetry, tossing about on oceans . . . Yet I am convinced that we all desire not to be corks tossing on an ocean; we desire to be poetic bodies, capable of having a point of view on our own destinies; on . . . humanity. On what makes humanity, its pains and its joys. Which is not the point of view of a cork . . . we no longer even know how to let ourselves feel, how to allow ourselves to feel as we feel. Nor how to accompany this feeling with the song that echoes it and restores it to us.
>
> (Cixous, in Cixous and Calle-Gruber 1997: 12)

The intention of my writing is to give both *permission* to the reader, and the discursive *means* of becoming the poetic body, who knows how to feel, and who can find the poetic means to express it.

I do not want to suggest that we can find a way of reading and writing that escapes subjection. Bodies are subjected. Bodies learn to recognize themselves through clichés. Bodies learn to separate mind from body. Yet bodies can also learn to use the very powers they gain through being subjected to turn their reflexive gaze on the discursive practices and the habituated ways of being that those practices make possible. That reflexive turn makes those practices both visible and revisable, and opens up the possibility of new ways of knowing. We take language up as our own in multiple ways, not in any simple linear or monolithic way. We have many modes of speaking and writing, many possible ways of knowing. It is amongst and within this complex web that one form of knowing can be used to trouble another.

We are subjected through discourses and within relations of power, and there is no clear boundary between what we are or are in process of becoming and those discourses through which we are subjected. But, as Deleuze (1995) points out, discourses/texts/thought are not static, any more than subjects are. In the very processes of becoming speaking, knowing subjects, we become subjects in transition, subjects who can use the powers that their subjection, by and through discourse, gives them, to trouble, to transform, to realign the very forces that shape them. We are subjected, we become human, and in that becoming can search out the possibilities for creative movement beyond the apparent fixity in the terms of our subjection.

I want the writing I do to trouble apparently intractable relations of power and the knowledges those relations presuppose and actualize, with a series of deconstructive moves that undermine the intractability of hierarchical and oppositional binaries such as male/female, mind/body, body/landscape. My task, as I see it, is to open up transformative possibilities through writing in such a way that the transformative potential is available to multiple and diverse readers, across disciplines, and both inside and outside of the academy.

The gap between intellectual knowledge and public knowledge is one that is always in process of being crossed and momentarily closed in multiple ways – through public broadcasting, through good journalism, through workshops in the community, through the teaching of our students and also by readers who take up our books and find that they can *play* what they find there. It is also possible to work with members of the community in collaborative projects, enabling them too to become 'specific intellectuals' (Foucault 2000b) in their own contexts (see, for example, Davies 1996). We should be very wary of constituting 'the public' as essentially ignorant, or as unable or unwilling to hear what we have to say. At the same time it is important to see how they are caught, as we are, in certain ways of constituting themselves and the world. They are implicated in the work we do, and we are not fundamentally separate from them in the ways the us/them, intellectual/public binary suggests. At the same time, it is important to question how and in what ways we can and do make our knowledge available to more than the ten or one hundred readers Foucault jokingly imagines. In order to pursue this question further, I want to place it historically, and in context, by asking what it means, currently, to be an intellectual, working in the academy.

Foucault proposed that the life of intellectuals has undergone a major shift from being the 'universal' intellectual in the nineteenth and early twentieth centuries to being the 'specific' intellectual of the late twentieth century. The universal intellectual was, above all, a writer who creates words in which all were able to 'recognize' and thus subject themselves. He (and it was usually a he) was 'the bearer of values and significations in which all can recognize themselves' (Foucault 2000b: 128). That so many of us managed to so recognize ourselves through the work of those elite white male 'universal' intellectuals is actually extraordinary, given how little relation the 'universals' often bore to our embodied selves. It is a testament to the human imagination, really, that we could do so. Moreover, it has been quite hard work to learn to undo the capacity to so recognize ourselves through those universals with which the world was constituted. Getting rid of the generic pronoun was a crucial step in enabling us to see how the 'he' who we thought had included us all, did not in fact do so (Davies 1987). Today's specific intellectual can no longer pretend to such universal knowledges. S/he works in local contexts with local issues, becomes an expert on a specific topic, being careful to specify its relevancies. The specific intellectual, Foucault says, no longer sets out to be the 'writer of genius' whose 'cry resounds even beyond the grave', though s/he has at his or her disposal 'powers that can either benefit or irrevocably destroy life. [S]he is no longer the rhapsodist of the eternal but the strategist of life and death' (Foucault 2000b: 129). Life and death, not just in relation to chemical and nuclear issues, but also in relation to human dignity and survival – land rights issues, violence, neglect and abuse of vulnerable groups of people, new forms of social organization and so on. Specific intellectuals, and in particular those who draw on poststructuralist theory, work on issues arising out of their own contexts, *and at the same time*, struggle after the textual/discursive insights that will enable them to escape being trapped in and limited by some aspects of the discourses that make up those specific contexts. And more, they must draw attention to the discourses themselves and their constitutive force, in particular, but not only, where that constitutive force is read as destructive (see, for example, Laws and Davies 2000). Alongside such deconstructive strategies, and deeply implicated in them, is a moral responsibility for reading the ways in which our deconstructive strategies work to transform, to open up or close down possibilities. Critique does not exist independently of transformation.

Whilst the specific intellectual does not adopt the god position and assume his or her words have ultimate power, it is nevertheless the case that writing is powerful, presupposing and actualizing knowledges, holding old knowledges in place or opening up the possibilities of new ways of seeing and being.

There are several weaknesses or dangers in the position of specific intellectuals, according to Foucault's (2000b) analysis. These are:

1 their vulnerability to being manipulated by those who control local struggles, such as political parties or trade unions;
2 their lack of a global strategy that links different groups working on related issues; and
3 their inability to gain outside support in the form of 'followers' who can give political currency to their ideas.

In relation to the first weakness we may be caught up in ways of seeing that are biased in ways we may or may not recognize at the time. In the second weakness, our knowledge may be produced in too limited a discursive field, failing to pick up and build from other disciplines. Lacking such insights we may miss out on alternative ways of seeing that would enable us to see the limitations of our own visions and the blind alleys we may have written ourselves into. The sum of the effects of these first two weaknesses may be knowledges that may be harmful (even death-dealing) in ways we do not anticipate. But even when we do not succumb to these weaknesses, taking up Foucault's third point, we may be positioned in such a way that we cannot necessarily gain the kind of public attention that enables our ideas to be heard and taken up. While we might develop incisive analyses of social or political movements, we may be unable to influence or prevent developments that our analyses, if heard or understood, would have precluded. Moreover, the very specificity of our knowledge may be such that we cannot bring it together with other fields of knowledge relevant to the political or bureaucratic decision being taken. We were, for example, unable to see the dangers inherent in the changes that were taking place in our very own places of work over the last decade. Neo-liberal forms of management have been (and are still being) introduced, with very little voicing of protest (Coady 2000; Rose 1999). And even if we had seen the dangers, and understood the effects of neo-liberalism, we may not have had a sufficient following to be able to halt the change.

Foucault suggests that we are at a point where 'the function of the specific intellectual needs to be reconsidered' (2000b: 130). His point is not that our work should be valued less in relation to the work of universal intellectuals, but rather that we should come to understand more clearly the relations between knowledge and power as we exercise them:

> these local specific struggles haven't been a mistake and haven't led to a dead end. One may even say that the role of the specific intellectual must become more and more important in proportion to the political responsibilities which [s]he is obliged willy-nilly to accept, as nuclear scientist, computer expert, pharmacologist, and so on. It would be a dangerous error to discount him[/her] politically in his[/her] specific relation to a local form of power, either on the grounds that this is a specialist matter that doesn't concern the masses (which is doubly wrong: they are already aware of it, and in any case implicated in it), or that the specific intellectual serves the interests of state or capital (which is true, but at the same time shows the strategic position [s]/he occupies; or, again, on the grounds that [s]/he propagates a scientific ideology (which isn't always true, and is anyway certainly a secondary matter compared with the fundamental point: the effects proper to true discourses).
>
> (Foucault 2000b: 130–1)

Since this interview with Foucault, which took place in 1976, the implementation of neo-liberal strategies of management in universities has intensified the negative possibilities that he envisaged. Funding for universities has been reduced in many countries, and academic research has been more closely tied to the interests of state and capital than ever before. Neo-liberal strategies are primarily strategies of surveillance, not so much through the conscience and consciousness of individual subjects, but through regimes of management in which rewards and punishments purport to control and manipulate desired 'outcomes'. Governments, more than ever, seek to manipulate universities through economic measures that are used to enforce specific management practices within universities. As the image of the universal intellectual vanishes, and specific intellectuals take their place, intellectuals are increasingly seen as subjects whose conduct can and should be conducted by governments.

It is against the grain of such trends that Foucault suggests that we abandon the task of responding 'correctly' and within the terms of the multiple discourses through which we are subjected. Instead we might work, he suggests, to find the strategies of power/knowledge through which it becomes possible to develop life into its own *telos* and with it, a capacity for critique. He does not see this as a simple task. The system is 'redoubtable', that is it is to be feared, it is formidable, and at the same time it is worthy of respect. Rose observes:

> [Foucault was] attracted to the Nietzschean opposition between two conceptions of morality and moral obligation. In the first form, which both he and Nietzsche found problematic, morality is obedience to a heteronomous code which we must accept, and to which we are bound by fear and guilt. In the second, morality is an exercise in ascetics, whereby through experimentation, exercise and permanent work on oneself one can make life into its own telos. Thomas Osborne has suggested that this is what Foucault had in mind when he advocated the transformation of life into a work of art – an ascetics based upon a work of freedom. Freedom, here, was not defined substantively but understood in terms of the constant exercise of detachment from culturally given codes in order to practice a life of constant moral experimentation.
>
> (Rose 1999: 96–7)

Foucault's position strongly approximates a familiar ideal of the life and responsibility of intellectuals in the academy. But the totalization or totalitarian rule Foucault writes about, which is central to neo-liberal forms of government, may hold intellectuals in positions that prohibit such struggles. Through a series of complex forms of reasoning, and many shifts in practice (shifts we accepted in the name of quality assurance and accountability), intellectual responsibility has been undermined and replaced with accountability, not to oneself or one's profession but to accountants and auditors (Rose 1999). Significant proportions of university funds and energies are diverted to the sacred cow of auditing. And yet the shaky base of figures and accounting, renowned for its capacity to be incorrect and misleading and to give false security, has, at the same time, been used as a tool for puncturing other forms of reason. Auditing, while espousing 'accountability' and transparency, actively sets up a culture of mistrust:

... these methods do not so much hold persons to account as create patterns of accountability. They create accountability to one set of norms – transparency, observability, standardization and the like – at the expense of accountability to other sets of norms. Indeed, accountability itself becomes a criterion of organizational health ...

Audits of various sorts have come to replace the trust that social government invested in professional wisdom and the decisions and actions of specialists. ... Power suggests that audit is a technology of mistrust, designed in the hope of restoring trust in organizational and professional competence. Yet it appears that the very technologies of mistrust perpetually fail to immunize the assemblages they govern from doubt ... the proliferation of audit serves only to amplify and multiply the points at which doubt and suspicion can be generated. Whilst audits have become key fidelity techniques in new strategies of government, they generate an expanding spiral of distrust of professional competence, and one that feeds the demand for more radical measures which will hold experts to account.

(Rose 1999: 154–5)

We are thus constituted through strategies that, in supposedly making us good, accountable citizens, undermine the very basis of our capacity to do our work and to reach the audiences who might take up the transformative potential in it. It would seem now, more than ever, that there is a need to enter into the second form of morality, that is, the 'exercise in ascetics, whereby through experimentation, exercise and permanent work on oneself one can make life into its own telos' (Rose 1999: 96–7). Or, in Cixous' terms, in which we become 'poetic bodies, capable of having a point of view on our own destinies; on. . . humanity. On what makes humanity, its pains and its joys' (Cixous, in Cixous and Calle-Gruber 1997: 12). We are individually and collectively responsible for a critique of those same forms of power that make our critique unable to be heard.

Finally ...

We may occasionally mourn the loss of the universal intellectual with all the certainty and security that his authoritative knowledges provided. But his demise was made inevitable by the unacknowledged specificity of his position within regimes of power and knowledge – he was specifically masculine and middle class and white (and possibly, though not necessarily, heterosexual). He counted these accumulated specificities as universal and took himself to be able to speak for us all. A poststructuralist approach makes it impossible to stand in such an apparently universal god-like position and get away with it for long. The intellectual has to acknowledge his or her specific location on any number of axes. At the same time there is a very real danger that today's intellectual will become dangerously narrow. S/he may become too facile in changing discourses, too pragmatic. Such facility is part and parcel of postmodern existence. Yet it has made us vulnerable to entering into unexamined discourses – playing within their terms, even seduced by them, only to find, as with economic rationalism and neo-liberalism, that we have lost sight of the things we are responsible for as intellectuals in our societies. So many managers have competently taken up these new discourses, only to find that there is no path back to a discourse of respect for professional knowledge or to a sense of ethical commitment to the work of the academy. The power/knowledge of economic rationalism and new managerialism precludes a valuing of intellectual work. These discourses do not stay isolated within management. By their very nature they infiltrate every aspect of academic life and become its *raison d'être*. Other discourses are marginalized, side-lined, made irrelevant. The work of the 70s and 80s was to dismantle knowledge/power as it was vested in universal intellectuals. The work of the 90s might be said to be the harnessing of specific intellectuals within economic rationalist and neo-liberal discourses. The work ahead of us is to make that harnessing visible, and to dismantle it – to make our way towards a responsible take-up and elaboration of specific knowledges. At the same time, any text is as plural as its readers, and it is in that plurality, and in the collaboration between readers and writers, that dissemination begins:

> The text is plural. This does not mean only that it has several meanings but that it fulfills the very plurality of meaning: an *irreducible* (and not just acceptable) plurality. The text is not coexistence of meaning, but passage, traversal; hence it depends not on an interpretation, however liberal, but an explosion, on dissemination.
>
> (Barthes 1986: 59)

PART III

9 | Developing informed practice for disseminating qualitative research

Christina Hughes

> Dissemination question: what 'is going on,' according to what time, what space, what structure, what becomes of the 'event' when 'I write,' . . .
>
> (Derrida 1993: 41)

I noted in the Introduction that a major purpose of this text was to develop informed practice in the field of dissemination. The choice of the term 'informed' was because of a number of concerns that I have with what is conveyed when we use the more common language of 'best practice'. These concerns are:

- Best practice guides portray an image that social relationships are amenable to change through the implementation of, say, ten simple bullet points. They, therefore, suggest it is possible to find simple solutions to what are, actually, often intractable and certainly highly complex social concerns.
- Best practice guides suggest that the user of the guide has power over those who are the focus of her implementation. After all, she holds the list in her hand!
- Although I do not believe this is the intention, best practice guides have a tendency to suggest that it is morally permissible to manipulate others and exercise this 'power over' others.

For example, the HEQE (2001) model, set out in Chapter 2, advises disseminators to focus on the needs and desires of the audience to whom they are disseminating. They might, for example, do this by telling good stories of 'what works' or giving examples of the successful use of an innovation when used by others. In effect, such advice can lead one to cynically believe that effective dissemination relies on some good sales talk that works by promising to fulfil the needs and desires, or solve the problems, of the purchaser. Indeed, as Chapter 1 indicated and Loraine Blaxter (in this volume) concludes, there is a move towards treating research as some form of saleable commodity. For example, the 'What works?' discourse of the UK government outlined in Chapter 1 is part of a wider move by governments to encourage academics to enter into alliances with industry on the basis that academic researchers can provide organizations with the information they require. As Bronwyn Davies (this volume and personal communication) notes, this creates a series of dilemmas for researchers. It assumes, for example, an apolitical set of industries or schools and an apolitical set of workers, teachers, administrators and so forth. It also assumes that knowledge is innocent in the sense that it fits within a realist frame in which no more than descriptive accounts of that reality can be provided. Such a situation renders researchers vulnerable to the perceptions of their industry partners and funders. For example, it seriously compromises a researcher's freedom to produce something unfamiliar or threatening to the already known or the politically acceptable. In addition, enormous distrust can arise when researchers do not produce material that accords with the predictable taken-for-granted worlds of those they research with and for.

As we saw in Chapter 2, the development of models of effective dissemination have a long heritage in positivist views of social reality. Interpretivist and critical accounts may have ameliorated these somewhat in the sense that they have highlighted the complexities, and in the case of critical accounts the politics, associated with the transfer and take-up of knowledge. However, the more recent demand for evidence-based knowledge, and in consequence evidence-based dissemination techniques, indicates the hegemonic nature of realist views of social reality. To repeat the words of Brown and Jones (2001: 169), none of these models challenge the 'singular dominant account'. This is a belief that research can tell us 'how it is' (Brown and Jones 2001: 169) so that we 'can then plan new strategies for the creation of new outcomes' (Brown and Jones 2001: 169).

For example, Huberman's (1994) interpretivist model of 'sustained interactivity' is concerned with the micro-relations between researcher and practitioner in order to bridge the academic-practitioner gap. Huberman focuses on the reciprocal conversations that develop and that enable each to understand the others' concerns. In terms of power relations, Huberman's model is one that suggests that the academic's role is one of service to the practitioner. Here, the academic's responsibility is to respond to practitioners' concerns through changes at a day-to-day level in the design, execution and potential outcomes of the research.

The general criticisms of Huberman's model are two-fold. First, because it is a model of *sustained* interactivity, it is based on small-scale projects that are labour-intensive and time-consuming. In a climate of more-for-less employment conditions, it is a problematic model for those concerned with generating generalizable solutions because to do so would require the employment, and associated investments, of considerable numbers of small teams. Secondly, although the researcher is clearly given a service role, the power relations already existing between those in the academy and those in, say, schools confine the practitioner to the role of client rather than full partner, let alone the producer or initiator of research. In consequence, if the aim is to (a) have a much wider dissemination and take-up of innovations and (b) shift the power balance from academic researcher to teacher practitioner, a new model is required.

This is where Hargreaves (1999) intercedes into the debate through what he terms Mode 2 knowledge. Using the terms transferability and transposability, Hargreaves' model seeks to take account of issues of context. For example, as teachers are well aware, what works with one class or in one institution may not work with or in another. For this reason, practice has to be fluid and context appropriate. Best practices, therefore, or useful innovations have to take this into account. Hargreaves suggests that this can be done through the development of heterogeneous networks of practitioners and academics that will form the basis of Mode 2 knowledge. At first hand, with its concern with the power hierarchy of academic-practitioner, it could be argued that Hargreaves' model shares many of the concerns of those working within critical models of research for social justice.

However, there are two key differences between Hargreaves' model and those developed for social justice. First, although Hargreaves does reach out a hand to the academic community by saying that their knowledge and skills are central to the successful implementation of Mode 2 knowledge, it is unclear whether he sees the future outcome of such a model in terms of a reversal of the traditional hierarchical relationship or as developing some kind of egalitarian partnership. Certainly, social justice models are generally very wary about social change that simply reverses who has 'power over' whom. Secondly, the type of knowledge that Hargreaves' model seeks to produce does not appear to concern itself with a broader questioning of the imperialistic nature of Western knowledge and its 'best' practices. In this, Hargreaves' model remains steadfastly close to a modernist and imperialistic version of social science that can produce appropriate technologies that will deliver specific outcomes based on Western positivist modes of thought.

It is here, therefore, that I turn to an analysis of the case studies presented in Part II of this text and what they can tell us about developing informed practices in the dissemination of qualitative research. None of the case studies in this volume assume knowledge to be apolitical. In consequence, they do not assume that dissemination is an apolitical process. Rather, they trouble dominant accounts of dissemination by troubling the nature of knowledge itself. There are three aspects to these case studies that I believe are particularly significant here and which will enable us to develop an understanding of the complexities and challenges of dissemination. First, what has been important about each of these case studies is the attention they have given to the subjective realm of dissemination. This 'involves the conscious and unconscious thoughts and emotions which constitute our senses of "who we are" and the feelings which are brought to different positions within culture' (Woodward 1997: 39). Such a focus adds an important critical dimension to the weight of objectivist models that form the majority of literature on dissemination. Secondly, the case studies have understood dissemination as an ethical and political process that has as its concern whose voices are heard and how knowledge is re-presented. In consequence, we have to understand informed practice in dissemination as something that is far more than a technical question. Thirdly, as reflections on experiences in the field, the case studies offer both practical and philosophical guidance for qualitative researchers who seek to disseminate their work. These issues are intertwined in the discussion that now follows.

The emotional realm of dissemination

There is something quite underdeveloped in the models presented in Chapter 2 of this text. This is that no attention appears to have been given to the emotional realm, and the personal, associated with dissemination acts. With their heritage in the detached scientism of positivism and the separation of body and mind of Cartesian rationality, this should perhaps come as no surprise. These models purport to represent human processes but they do so by writing out the realm of feeling that is so central to being human. Indeed, Bronwyn Davies offers us an important insight here in respect of dissemination and the assumptions of a mind-body separation. She calls on us to notice that the word disseminate derives from the word semen and, in consequence, is a fundamentally embodied term. Yet, we commonly understand the processes of dissemination as requiring disembodied acts through which ejaculated knowledge forms itself into something that is separate from each of us. As the papers in this volume testify, this is not the case. Rather we are emotionally, subjectively and politically invested in the dissemination acts of which we are part. Loraine Blaxter comments in this respect that we are caught up in 'the chain, circle or chaos of dissemination' of which we are both objects and subjects.

Certainly, there is strong attention to issues of emotion and feeling in Loraine's paper. Loraine speaks of experiencing shame at being re-presented in a travel guide as the orientalist that she had so strongly rejected. Similarly, Tuula Gordon illustrates how a newspaper article that misrepresented her research had emotional impacts on all of those concerned with the research by causing pain. These emotional impacts affected both researchers and respondents. Chris Mann's paper explores issues of feeling as she documents the frustrations of an organizational researcher who is endeavouring to disseminate findings in a bureaucratic environment. She also discusses how her position as a working-class woman in an elite, masculine institution raised issues of credibility and, in consequence, worked against her with some audiences in terms of how her findings might be heard. Not being heard is also a strong theme in Carrie Paechter's paper. Here she evidences strong concern, and a similar sense of frustration, at not being able to disseminate her work to those she believes would benefit. Finally, Becky Francis's work demonstrates how postmodern critiques of emancipatory ideas present a challenging emotional climate through which we need to work out where we stand and what we stand for. Bronwyn's comment that writing is an intensely personal process highlights these points. As she reflects, writing, and I would add all other forms of dissemination, are not produced through discursive contexts that are somehow separate from our embodied selves or our innermost passions and desires. Rather writing, and other forms of dissemination, are integral to these aspects of self.

In addition, these issues of emotion and subjectivity cannot be separated from the intellectual investments that occur through engaging in ongoing and changing debates that surround the nature and purposes of research. One issue that has had a major impact in this respect is how we understand the nature of knowledge or, as it is termed, epistemology. The writing in of emotion, as is the case here, as essential to understanding and developing informed knowledge of dissemination is one aspect of these debates. In terms of the case studies presented in this text, two further linked issues are salient. These are the challenge of 'post' epistemologies and the ethics of representation.

The challenge of 'post' epistemologies

This text draws on three forms of 'post' critique. These are postmodernism, postcolonialism and poststructuralism. All three are contested terms and, as Finlayson (1999: 149) comments in respect of postmodernism, defining these terms is an 'appropriately difficult exercise'. Indeed, Weedon (1999) notes that postmodernism is often conflated with poststructuralism. This is because debates about universality, subjectivity and power overlap in postmodernist and poststructuralist thought. Beasley (1999) suggests that one way of understanding the distinction between postmodernism and poststructuralism is to view poststructuralism as a sub-set of postmodernism. Within such a view, poststructuralism remains concerned about universality, subjectivity and power through a focus on the workings of discourse and language.

As with other 'post' terminologies, when we consider postcolonialism we have to take account of two meanings of the term 'post'. In common with other assumptions surrounding this term, some readings suggest that post-colonialism refers chronologically to the period after colonialization. Other readings imply that postcolonialist writing is that which is opposed to, and resists, colonialism. Certainly, as I have identified elsewhere (Hughes, 2002a) postcolonialism can be understood in terms of:

- The critique of colonialist modes of representation in Western research and related issues of voice; which are problematized through
- An emphasis on multiple differences, complex diversities and locationality arising from issues of cultural hybridity and diasporic experiences, but;
- A cautionary retention of the importance of a unified political identity.

The challenges posed to research and dissemination by these 'post' epistemologies are manifold and are explored both here and below. Generally, postmodern critiques have called all empirical research into question. This is the focus of Becky Francis's discussion of dissemination. In particular, Becky discusses postmodern approaches in terms of their impact on feminist, qualitative, research. There are four aspects to this that Becky raises. First, postmodern theory has questioned the emancipatory nature of such research. For example, in Western societies, more women are entering the paid labour force. However, as women, we simultaneously remain primarily responsible for domestic care. Therefore, it *could* be said that all feminist activism has produced is the double shift. Is this emancipation? Secondly, postmodernism has questioned the idea of universal truths. Within feminism, a key aspect of this has been to deconstruct the idea of 'woman' as a universal category. In particular, feminist debates have been concerned to highlight how 'woman' is a category marked by issues of age, 'race', class, sexuality and disability. The result of this is that feminism cannot claim to speak for *all* women. Thirdly, postmodernism has challenged the concept of reality. Here, the notions of a positivistic 'real' reality or a constructed, interpretive reality are overwritten by a textual concept of reality through which, for some, the very concept of reality is an anachronism. Fourthly, postmodernism has asked us to reconsider ideas of truth and it has certainly challenged Truth with a capital 'T'. This is, in part, because we know that there are competing versions of what we understand as truth or fiction, real or fact. How can we decide what is True? Overall, therefore, as Norris (1999: 29, emphasis in original) notes in relation to the work of Lyotard, postmodernist thought suggests that:

> . . . we nowadays need to make sense of our lives in a context of multiple, open ended, ever proliferating narratives and language games. We tell many stories about ourselves, about history, philosophy, the human and the nature sciences, and of course about politics and the various lessons to be drawn from past political events. But the chief lesson, Lyotard says, is that we have to respect the narrative

differend and not make the error – the typical 'Enlightenment' error – of believing any one such story to possess superior truth-telling warrant.

(Norris 1999: 29)

In terms of dissemination, this means that it could be argued that all research is doing is producing stories. In such a situation 'Do we really need to do empirical research at all?' Becky's response is an emphatic yes. Becky comments on how she is unwilling to accept a relativist perception of the world where there are only stories and where it is not possible to decide which stories are better than others. Here, she draws our attention to the material actualities of life through which issues of sex, 'race', class, age and disability make their impact. Becky's position rests on a rejection of postmodern ideas of the human being as totally constructed through discourse or text and, in consequence, as unable to exercise choice or agency. Rather, Becky takes up what is called a both/and position (see Hughes 2002b) whereby one recognizes how we are contradictory and complex beings, determined to some extent by discursive forces, but we are also able to resist these discourses.

In exploring issues of truth and story, Becky draws on her own research with schoolchildren and notes how, on the one hand, children very strongly reject the idea of stereotypical gender roles whereas, on the other hand, their behaviour often replicated these. Becky asks, therefore, whether we should regard these children's views as fiction. In other words, despite these children saying that they did not believe in gender stereotypes really they did! Both in ethical terms and in terms of the development of knowledge, Becky responds by saying that this is not the best way to look at the issue. Rather we should not be so disrespectful to respondents as to dismiss their stated opinions and beliefs. We should also cease being concerned with whether, or not, we are getting at the 'real truth'. Instead we should be using their responses to provide new insights into our research concerns. In this case 'What is it about gender stereotypes that evinces such passionate views from children?'

Debates about truth and story clearly have implications both in terms of what, and how, research findings are disseminated. Here Becky reflects on how the results of research will be dependent on the interactive nature of relationships in the field. We know, for example, that issues of 'race' or gender can impact on the course of an interview and in consequence on the type of data produced. This means that it is not possible to produce one 'true' version of events. The researcher's responsibility, therefore, lies in striving, through dissemination, to recognize the limitations of research and openly declaring the material factors that impact upon the perspective that we are disseminating. They also lie in recognizing that what gets disseminated is as important as how it is disseminated.

The ethics of representation

> We are now totally surrounded by representations. As meaning-creating creatures we employ concepts – thoughts about what the world is 'really' like – and we express those thoughts in representative form, primarily through language. Representation thus mediates between our thought and reality. We would like to think that there is clarity to representation, so that there is no gap between thought and reality but a perfect correspondence. But representation suggests the re-presenting of something, looking at aspects of the world and then re-presenting them to us in a different way. This implies that a representation is one version of the world, not a real or simple reflection of reality. We might even say that representation could have a determining effect on our thought
>
> (Finlayson 1999: 148)

In Chapter 2, I gave the example of Kaupapa Maori approaches to research and dissemination. What was important within the Kaupapa Maori model was the issue of integrity to the values and ethics of Maori culture. The model presented by Smith (1999) was concerned to develop a different form of knowledge. This was one that was based upon Maori ways of knowing the social world. As Bishop (1998: 200) comments, this has been important because 'traditional research has misrepresented Maori understandings and ways of knowing by simplifying, conglomerating, and commodifying Maori knowledge for "consumption" by colonizers'. This has led to a misrepresentation of Maori experiences and to a denial of Maori authenticity and voice.

The development of Kaupapa Mauri research has required Maori peoples to design and implement research that was central to their concerns. Certainly, through dissemination, some fairly familiar themes arise such as networking and the sharing of knowledge. However, these are enacted within Maori cultural mores and social rules that, for example, privilege face-to-face meetings. They are also enacted within an ethic of self-determination, decolonization and social justice.

Nevertheless, the development of new models of research and dissemination do not, at a stroke, overcome intractable issues of voice and representation. Bishop comments in this respect that Kaupapa Maori ways of knowing are 'constantly under attack within Aotearoa/New Zealand from a wide front' (Bishop 1998: 212). Through political commitments and an awareness of the debates that surround issues of self-determination, issues of voice and representation were central to the case studies in this text. The concerns here are not only 'Who is permitted to speak on behalf of whom?' (Brooks 1997b: 110) but also acknowledging that 'there is a fine balance between showing solidarity with oppressed groups and assuming a position where one claims to speak on behalf of that group' (Brooks 1997b: 110). In this respect, developing an informed understanding of dissemination requires us to ask 'How are we being heard?' 'Who listens?' 'And why?' It also requires us to explore the reasons why we are 'Not being heard'.

How are we being heard?

The general issues raised by the Kaupapa Maori research model are resonant in Loraine's discussion of dissemination. Loraine uses the phrase 'Representational anxiety' to portray the tenor of debates within her discipline of social anthropology and through which two key questions are asked: 'Who are we speaking for?' and 'How are we re-presented when we are speaking for?' Loraine notes how anthropology has faced a number of dilemmas that are resonant in the critiques raised by Kaupapa Maori, and other, postcolonial researchers. For example, through the production of 'travellers' tales', anthropology is associated with the politics of colonialism. As a consequence, anthropology has experienced moral doubt because of its concern that research should be, as Loraine calls it, decent. In addition, the debates within the ethics of fieldwork have highlighted how anthropological research has the ability to uncover problems but this does not necessarily mean it can solve them.

Loraine uses the trigger of a travel guide, and the theme of memory, to explore how disseminated products from her research challenged the sense of self-identity she had carried with her of the socially responsible 'good' researcher and, indeed, thought she was recreating through the dissemination of her research. Here, Loraine discusses how, many years after the completion of her PhD, she 'remembers' seeing that a travel guide had replicated some of the findings from her research on villagers in the French Pyrenees. She notes how she was at first delighted to see that her ideas were being taken up and how she then experienced horror at how the people of the Pyrenees were represented in the travel guide. In particular, the travel guide portrayed a particularly negative conceptualization of these villagers by suggesting that gift-giving – a theme central to her PhD dissertation – was anachronistic social behaviour located in out-dated ways of behaving. Gift-giving, therefore, became a curiosity for the gaze of the traveller rather than a fairly common and ordinary experience.

This example from Loraine's work indicates how we cannot control how our research will be re-presented. Yet her experience is not uncommon. As a researcher working within critical paradigms, Tuula also is concerned that neither she, nor her research, is viewed as critical of the individuals who are the subjects of her work. Thus, she may want to raise a critique of contemporary politics and policies in education but this does not mean that she sees teachers as simply agents of the state. However, as Tuula notes, this is not necessarily how others will re-present her research. Tuula uses an example of media exposure to demonstrate how issues and themes drawn on within legitimate analytic frameworks can be taken up and re-presented in a negative way. Thus, the term 'jail' that is used in a metaphoric way in academic papers to explore the subjective realm of school is taken as an empirical reality. As Tuula comments 'There is a difference in saying school "is a jail" as a newspaper reported and saying it is "*like* a jail" as their research reported.' The former is a statement. The latter is a metaphor. The metaphor crystallizes one, often invisible, story whilst hiding others. Whilst school is '*like*' a jail, it may also be a place where important informal relations are forged.

The concern with how we are heard is not confined to researchers and their outputs. Those who are the subjects of our research will also have investments, of both a subjective and material kind, in how they are represented. Chris Mann's study of elite groups and dissemination processes highlights how such groups seek to control how their own, or their organization's, image is portrayed. Chris notes how elite groups will be sensitive to losing face or will see their control over image jeopardized by researchers whose actions they cannot control. In consequence, they may seek to prevent researcher access in the first place. When they do allow access, the issue of image, and consequent control, become central to which, if any, aspects of the research are disseminated.

Though it may not be welcome, it is not unusual for researchers to face varied kinds of pressures in relation to the dissemination of their work. For example, as a contracted researcher several years ago, I was required to sign a confidentiality document that prevented me from publishing any findings from the work I was doing. More recently, the Times Higher Educational Supplement (March 8, 2002: 11) published a survey of 800 members of the lecturers' union Natfhe. This suggested that one in ten academics have been put under pressure to alter, suppress or delay findings. 30 per cent of those who had experienced such pressures reported that these were applied by the funding source.

In this respect, Chris demonstrates how the concerns of an organization over how it might be represented impact on the dissemination process in a series of ways. For example, the committee structure of an organization can cause serious practical problems in terms of time delays and procrastination. The concern for image can lead to increasing restrictions being placed on the release of material so that, finally, it only becomes disseminated to a small inner circle. In addition, committees see that their role is to take charge of the dissemination process in its entirety and so leave the researcher with no control whatsoever over what, or how, findings are disseminated or, indeed, whether their name appears on the cover of reports.

Finally, it is perhaps salutary to note that whilst those with institutional power are able to shape the dissemination process, other subjects of research are not in such a position. Generally, ethical research codes are designed to offer protection to research participants. The basic principles of ethical codes highlight the importance of adequately informing potential research participants of the nature of the research and its likely impact in their lives. Ethical codes urge researchers to ensure that they have gained informed consent and that they respect the privacy of the individual. Although limited in their effect, the most common way of protecting individuals and organizations is through the use of pseudonyms. Yet, Becky raises an important issue in terms of the ethics of representation. This is that children who take part in research often do not want to be anonymized. Rather, part of the fun and excitement of being involved is the possibility of seeing their names in print. In such circumstances, does the researcher respect their right to refuse a pseudonym or does she exert her authority and power 'in the child's best interests'?

Who listens? and why?

In Chapter 2 I noted that there was a debate in respect of how dissemination should be defined. On the one hand, there were those who argue that dissemination is a deliberate and systematic process and the spread of knowledge in any other way cannot be labelled as such. On the other hand, there are those who argue that a more widespread diffusion of knowledge can be understood as an aspect of dissemination. The problem with debates of this kind is that they urge us to make a choice between two opposing alternatives as if there are no other options or as if we cannot choose both. For example, I have commented that the nature of qualitative research, in respect of getting close to the researched, brings its own dilemmas and opportunities in respect of the spread of knowledge and ideas. Whilst some may call this diffusion, it would appear that the outcome is the same. This is that ideas, knowledges and practices are, or are not, taken up.

Loraine's autobiographical account offers one example of the refusal to name the take-up of knowledge as either diffusion or dissemination. Loraine describes how her intellectual life, often at the margins of the academy, has been sustained by conversations with friends and the giving, and receiving, of books. In this way she built up and maintained her knowledge of debates in the academy. She notes that the texts on her shelf, therefore, were no coincidence and were not, as it may appear, the result of a windborn process of diffusion. But, also, they were not the result of a systematic and planned dissemination. In this way, Loraine demonstrates how we have to take account of not only 'Who listens?' but why they might do so. For Loraine, her bookshelf represents the listening in on debates that resonated with her political consciousness and some subject positions. These voices were of exile, movement, marginality and alliances.

Tuula's paper also reflects on how 'Who listens?' is related to an audience's subjective investments in the subject matter of dissemination. Here, she discusses how dissemination can link to past events in the listener's/reader's life. For example, Tuula discusses how more-for-less employment economies place intolerable pressures on teachers to produce 'results'. This can also result in pressure being placed on children to produce those results. Tuula is conscious that listeners/readers might, wrongly, interpret this pressure on children as the teacher's fault. This is because they might, for example, reflect back on the issues and feelings of their own or their children's schooling and, rather than seeing these as structurally and politically produced, simply see it as a consequence of teacher's bad management or stress.

These examples not only draw continuing attention to the realm of the subjective in the dissemination of research but also to the place of talk as an aspect of dissemination. Both Loraine and Tuula note that there has been very little attention given to the role, and ethics, of talk as a dissemination act. This is because work on dissemination has primarily been undertaken in an academic domain and here more value is given to the written products of research. Although, as Loraine notes, talk is an important aspect of dissemination amongst community groups, academic researchers are required to publish in internationally respected journals and are required to produce reports and synopses for funders and end-users. In this way, writing, and indeed reading, are seen to be superior to talk if we want to disseminate knowledge. Yet, much research is disseminated through lectures, class teaching, conference papers and through gossip. And, as Chris notes, research is disseminated internationally through email attachments and locally through chats in coffee bars.

Such a feature of dissemination is noted in good practice guides where researchers are encouraged to focus on their presentation skills and to ensure that their material is relevant to their audience. However, Tuula raises a serious issue in respect of best practice guides that encourage researchers to engage their audiences through the use of amusing anecdotes. Humour can bring people 'on side' and can leaven the more heavy-weight nature of research analysis. Even so, the researcher is left with an ethical dilemma. Thus, Tuula asks 'When does humour serve to re-present the subjects of an enquiry in negative or disingenuous ways?' For qualitative researchers, the subjects of research are not detached, statistical equations but are flesh and blood, real people. Relationships in the field blur the distinctions between stranger-friend and insider-outsider and researchers will, and do, feel a commitment to the relationships of trust and respect that are built up during fieldwork. Understood in this way, the amusing anecdote that serves to engage a potentially disinterested or bored audience, or spice up a lengthy lecture, becomes a cynical deployment of events in an individual's life. Certainly, the researcher knows to whom she is referring even though pseudonyms might be used. At the level of feeling and subjectivity, therefore, on such occasions the researcher can experience much ambivalence and unease. For Tuula, this means she avoids using the startling or negative slice of data.

Not being heard

Chapters 1 and 2 of this text highlight how there is great concern for academics to disseminate their materials more widely and more thoroughly. Indeed, it would be easy, when reading that literature, to believe that the majority of academics have no desire to leave their ivory towers and soil their hands by contact with 'real' people. However, as both Carrie and Chris point out, despite their huge commitment to reach those audiences for whom their work is designed, they face an enormous problem. This is that they are not being heard. How can we understand this resistance? Both Carrie and Chris draw on the problem of challenging orthodox knowledges.

In terms of an enormous commitment to dissemination, Carrie notes that because she believes that her research on gender and education can make a significant contribution, she is highly concerned to reach the potential audiences for her research. She also has access to her audience and, indeed, shares aspects of their identity. This is because she is a mother, with children at school and her audience is parents with similarly aged children. Yet, Carrie faces a dilemma. This is that of resistance to the messages of her research. Carrie explores this resistance in terms of how parenthood is constructed around particular ways of understanding the child.

Carrie explores this in respect of two subject positions. This is that of being an academic researcher and being a mother. Unlike Loraine, who discusses dissemination in respect of her marginality to the academy, Carrie reflects on how she feels a central part of academic life. For Carrie, 'being an academic' is fundamentally bound up with carrying out high-level, original academic research. Carrie, therefore, values her ability to write and speak in specialist registers, use particular vocabularies and understand key issues of the field. Indeed, although she recognizes that these languages and knowledges are exclusionary, the pleasure they give her means that she wants everyone to have them too. In addition Carrie notes how it is important to feel valued in one's work and that a key purpose of research, and, therefore, her sense of self, is the ability to make a difference. In consequence, Carrie believes that research should reach those for whom it might be useful. This includes parents. However, paradoxically, Carrie's access to parents and the sharing of her knowledge is conditional on her denying these very aspects of her identity

It is here that Carrie turns to a consideration of being a mother. She explores how, in their shaping of what is means to be a mother, childcare texts place enormous value on the idea that parents know what is best for their child. This is because such texts place considerable emphasis on viewing children as unique individuals. Carrie notes that this has three implications. First, where a parent's perceptions of their child conflict with an 'expert' opinion, expert knowledge can be dismissed as irrelevant to their particular child. Secondly, there is a strong taboo against criticizing someone else's parenting skills. Indeed, according to Backett (1982), parents are themselves unwilling to make unfavourable judgements about their own children. They would, therefore, always attribute problems or poor behaviour to a stage or phase appropriate to the child's development. Thirdly, when there is conflict between an expert and parental view, the expert's view will be dismissed on the grounds that they do not have sufficient practical knowledge or experience of childrearing. Overall, therefore, this means that when it comes to challenging prevailing orthodoxies parents are an incredibly difficult group to reach.

Using two stories from the school gates Carrie explores what this means for dissemination. The first is that of choosing a primary school for her sons. Here, Carrie notes how, although she had 'expert' research-based knowledge that informed her choice, interest from parents about her choice of school was sustained only as long as she could give 'gut' explanations. For example, that she didn't like the head teacher. Carrie comments that as soon as she raised issues concerned with the curriculum, approaches to teaching and the general organization of the school, people switched off. The second story relates to the spread of ideas disseminated through a text by Biddulph (1997) concerned with raising boys. Biddulph's ideas, contrary to those held by Carrie, strongly keyed in with conventional biologically based views of gender. It became a best seller and circulated rapidly amongst parents of Carrie's acquaintance. Whilst Carrie could marshall a series of arguments to counter the assertions made by Biddulph, she notes that if she raised these in conversation she was effectively viewed as breaking a taboo. Because parents were following the advice of Biddulph in the care of their children, Carrie could be viewed as challenging their childcare practices. At the school gate, therefore, the expert-self has to be negated or personal relationships with those who are also our friends are severely challenged.

The problem of resistance to knowing that Carrie's paper highlights is also resonant in Chris's paper. Here, Chris draws attention to a central issue in the politics of method. This is how quantitative, statistical approaches are not only considered to be the normal or usual way that social research is conducted but also that, when compared to qualitative approaches, they are seen to be superior. In the politics of what is counted as valid and trustworthy knowledge there is no doubt that the quantitative approach, with its Enlightenment hallmarks and aura of scientific detachment and objectivity, remains in primary position. In consequence, there is a tendency that qualitative approaches continue to be seen as soft, feminine, not 'real' research and lacking in credibility. The disseminated products of such research can, therefore, also be viewed as inconsequential, anecdotal, biased and subjective. For evidence of this we need only look to David Blunkett's remarks in respect of the development of educational research in the UK noted in Chapter 1. Certainly he gave some recognition of the role of qualitative research in developing insights into social processes. But, in actuality, he gave qualitative research the role of the supporting act. The star of the methodological show is to be evidence-based, large-scale quantitative research.

This is the terrain that Chris Mann's paper explores. Chris notes that because it is commonplace to think quantitative surveys are the only, or the best, way of undertaking research, qualitative research is a mystery to many people. Chris notes that, before dissemination of the findings can proceed, the researcher's role includes an educational one that involves demonstrating the value of the qualitative approach. Chris concludes on a positive note in this respect in terms of the potential reception of sceptical audiences to the value of qualitative research. However, she also offers some thoughtful advice on the extent of preparation in respect of what qualitative researchers might expect, or otherwise, from their audiences when they go to teach the qualitative method.

Secondly, the nature of qualitative data raises some important issues for dissemination in a time-poor society. The issue of lack of time was raised in several of the case studies and is an issue that has also been noted in the Hillage Report (Hillage et al. 1998). What is clear from the case studies is that it is not only researchers who face problems but also hard-pressed teachers and educational practitioners. In this respect, Chris notes that personnel in organizations require brief, accessible synopses of the key issues or findings. However, the size and nature of qualitative data means that reports can be long and cumbersome. Whilst the researcher may understand these conditions of production and strive to meet them, Chris asks us to consider how amenable qualitative data is to achieving this. For example, the requirement that the findings are presented in terms of statistical or aggregated patterns denies the subtlety of findings produced by qualitative data. Yet, this is a key strength of qualitative approaches. In addition, the short and telling anecdote replicates the issues raised by Tuula Gordon in terms that such anecdotes can both misrepresent the individuals who were the subjects of the research and can challenge the integrity of the researcher's relationships to the researched.

Moving beyond dissemination?

The foregoing has illustrated both the complexity of dissemination processes and that there are no quick and simple answers to the ethical, epistemological and representational concerns that dissemination acts give rise to. In such a situation, as with postmodern thinking more generally, one can too easily be led into a situation of stasis. Here, one stagnates in a quagmire of doubt unsure of how to proceed, and there lies the way to inaction, individualism and a lack of political consciousness. Yet, none of the contributors to this volume would accept such a situation. In this respect, we need to consider how we can move beyond present ways of knowing dissemination and towards new possibilities.

The final model discussed in Chapter 2 was focused on a deconstructive approach. This model sought to illustrate how certain conceptions of dissemination become privileged in contemporary methodological and policy discourses. In particular, this model demonstrates how dissemination is viewed mainly as a formal, discrete, technical, apolitical and final act of research. In consequence, other ways of knowing dissemination in qualitative research are put into the background. To demonstrate this my work with colleagues (Barnes et al. 2003) focused on the common processes of undertaking qualitative research and rewrote them as acts of dissemination. The literature review, therefore, becomes understood in terms of the take-up of disseminated ideas. The dialogic nature of interviews and fieldwork in qualitative approaches provides for moments of dissemination as those involved in the research act upon the substance of everyday conversations and comments. In highlighting these features of research, we hoped to draw into discourse the less status-rich side of the binaried meanings of dissemination. This work accords with critical frameworks of research where the purposes of deconstructive models are political.

In this respect, Bronwyn remarks how she wants her writing to trouble seemingly intractable relations of power and knowledge and to open up transformative possibilities. In this, she draws on Foucault's discussion of the universal and specific intellectual and explores what it means to be an intellectual working in the academy in the context of deprofessionalizing, long hour cultures, more-for-less economies, outcomes-based funding and 'quality' audits. Indeed, the spectre of the universal intellectual has inhabited the foregoing discussion through the concern to challenge what he stood for. The universal intellectual, like the universal subject, presented himself as the bearer of all our values and could assume to speak for all. As Bronwyn notes, and as the foregoing testifies, the intellectual can no longer pretend to such universal knowledges. Rather, the specific intellectual works in local contexts with local knowledges and is careful to specify the parameters of her work.

However, Bronwyn comments that the specific intellectual faces a number of dangers. For example, because the postmodern condition emphasizes the fragmentary, spasmodic, multiple nature of the self, s/he may become too pragmatic and too easy in changing discourses. In this, she might believe that values, modes of operation and personal politics can be slipped on as easily as selecting clothes from a wardrobe. Bronwyn notes that many managers have taken up new discourses of 'quality', accountability and empowerment without examining them carefully. What they find is that there is no way back to a discourse of respect for professional knowledge. In addition, through many forms of reasoning and shifts in practice, intellectual responsibility has been replaced with accountability to accountants and auditors. And, paradoxically, the seeming 'transparency' that is associated with accountability has led to a culture of mistrust.

In consequence, Bronwyn reflects that we are constituted in strategies that undermine the bases of our work and, therefore, undermine our capacities to reach audiences who might take up the transformative potential of our research. In such environments, therefore, there is a danger of losing sight of the things we are responsible for in our societies. In particular, this is that we are individually, and collectively, responsible for a critique of those same forms of power that make our critique unable to be heard.

Bronwyn's paper, with its attention to ascetics, experimentation and multiplicity of meaning, is offered as an example of the transformative possibilities of dissemination. Through her poetry, Bronwyn asks us to unfold rather than close down the meanings in her paper. In this respect, Sargisson's (1996) commentary on the notion of utopianism is useful for the analogies we can make with regard to the field of dissemination. Sargisson notes how blueprints for utopias convey some kind of perfect resolution and represent a closing down of other options. With great similarity to a 'best practice' document, once one has produced a utopian model it can appear that there is nothing left to discuss. In consequence, Sargisson argues for an open-ended conceptualization of utopia that is perceived as a dynamic and unending process.

The same should be said of dissemination. Models that are produced of the dissemination process have a tendency to conflate the 'is' and the 'ought'. They therefore explore the practices of research communication and change in terms of how it 'is' and then proceed to respond with a finessed model of how it 'ought' to be. In other words, how one can 'do' dissemination better. The contributors to this volume have each challenged this notion of dissemination as a final, perfect, apolitical, technical-rational act. This is because they have challenged the very meanings of knowledge itself. In so doing, they have unfolded the meanings of dissemination, and the production of knowledge, in qualitative research in ways we have yet to know.

References

Acker, S. (1981) No Woman's Land: British Sociology of Education 1960–1979, *Sociological Review*, 29(1): 77–104.

Acker, S. (1994) *Gendered Education*. Buckingham: Open University Press.

Adler, P. and Adler, P. (1993) Ethical issues in self-censorship: ethnographic research in sensitive topics, in C. Renzetti and R. Lee (eds) *Researching Sensitive Topics*. Newbury Park, CA: Sage.

Aiken, S. (1989) Writing (in) Exile: Isak Dinesen and poetics of displacement, in M. Broe and A. Ingram (eds) *Women's Writing in Exile*. London: Chapel Hill.

Ang-Lygate, M. (1996) Waking From a Dream of Chinese Shadows, *Feminism & Psychology*, 6(1): 56–60.

Assiter, A. (1996) *Enlightened Women: Modernist Feminism in a Postmodern Age*. London: Routledge.

Backett, K. (1982) *Mothers and Fathers*. London: MacMillan.

Bailey, F. (ed.) (1971) *Gifts and Poison: The Politics of Reputation*. Oxford: Blackwell.

Bailyn, L. (2001) Gender Equity in Academia: Lessons from the MIT Experience. Occasional paper 2, The Athena Project, Equality Challenge Unit.

Balbus, I. (1987) Disciplining women: Michel Foucault and the power of feminist discourse, in S. Benhabib and D. Cornhill (eds) *Feminism as Critique*. Cambridge: Polity Press.

Barlow, J., France, L. and Hayes-Farmer, N. (2000) Disseminating Good Practice: The Role of the Internal Learning and Teaching Conference, *Innovations in Education and Training International*, 37(4): 356–360.

Barnes, V., Clouder, L., Hughes, C., Purkis, J. and Pritchard, J. (2003) Deconstructing Dissemination: Dissemination as Qualitative Research, *Qualitative Research*, 3(2).

Barthes, R. (1986) *The Rustle of Language*. Berkeley: The University of California Press.

Ben-Peretz, M. (1994) The Dissemination and Use of Research Knowledge in Teacher Education Programs: A Nonevent? *Knowledge and Policy: International Journal of Knowledge Transfer and Utilization*, 7(4): 108–117.

BERA (1998) Turmoil and Opportunity, *Research Intelligence*, no. 66, October. www.bera.ac.uk/ri/no66/ri66editor.html.

Berger, J. (1979) *Pig Earth*. London: Writers and Readers Co-operative.

Biddulph, S. (1997) *Raising Boys*. London: Thorsons.

Bird, B. and Allen, D. (1989) Faculty Entrepreneurship in Research University Environments, *Journal of Higher Education*, 60(5): 583–596.

Blaxter, L. (1971a) Rendre service and Jalousie, in F. Bailey (ed.) *Gifts and Poison: The Politics of Reputation*, pp.119–138. Oxford: Basil Blackwell.

Blaxter, L. (1971b) The politics of development: social change in a French Pyrenean commune. Unpublished DPhil Dissertation, University of Sussex, Falmer.

Blaxter, L. (2000) Voluntary participation and involvement in adult education: a reflection on teacher responsibility and student withdrawal, *Journal of Access and Credit Studies*, 2(1): 33–44.

Blaxter, L. and Hughes, C. (2000) Social capital: a critique, in J. Thompson (ed.) *Stretching the Academy*. Leicester: NIACE.

Blaxter, L., Hughes, C. and Tight, M. (2001) *How to Research*, 2nd edn. Buckingham: Open University Press.

Blunkett, D. (2000) *Influence or Irrelevance: Can Social Science Improve Government?* www.bera.ac.uk/ri/no71/ri71blunkett.html.

Boyne, R. (1990) *Foucault and Derrida: The Other Side of Reason*. London: Unwin Hyman.

Brooks, A. (1997a) *Academic Women*. Buckingham: Open University Press/SRHE.

Brooks, A. (1997b) *Postfeminisms: Feminism, Cultural Theory and Cultural Forms*. London: Routledge.

Brown, H. (1992) *Women Organising*. London: Routledge.

Brown, S. (1994) Research in Education: What Influence on Policy and Practice? *Knowledge and Policy: International Journal of Knowledge Transfer and Utilization*, 7(4): 94–107.

Brown, T. and Jones, L. (2001) *Action Research and Postmodernism: Congruence and Critique*. Buckingham: Open University Press.

Burman, E. (1992) Developmental Psychology and the Postmodern Child, in J. Doherty, E. Graham and M. Malek (eds) *Postmodernism and the Social Sciences*. Basingstoke: MacMillan.

Burman, E. (1994) *Deconstructing Developmental Psychology*. London: Routledge.

Cameron, A. (1986) *Daughters of Copperwomen*. Vancouver: Women's Press.

Carette, J. (ed.) (1999) *Religion and Culture*. New York: Routledge.

Cealey Harrison, W. (2001) Truth is Slippery Stuff, in B. Francis and C. Skelton (eds) *Investigating Gender: Contemporary Perspectives in Education*. Buckingham: Open University Press.

Cealey Harrison, W. and Hood-Williams, J. (2001) *Beyond Sex and Gender*. London: Sage.

Cixous H. and Calle-Gruber, M. (1997) *Hélène Cixous Rootprints. Memory and Life Writing*. New York: Columbia University Press.

Clifford, J. and Marcus, G. (eds) (1986) *Writing Culture: The Poetics and Politics of Ethnography*. Berkeley: University of California Press.

Coady, T. (ed.) (2000) *Why Universities Matter*. Sydney: Allen and Unwin.

Coffey, A. (1999) *The Ethnographic Self: Fieldwork and the Representation of Identity*. London: Sage.

Cohen, L., Manion, L. and Morrison, K. (2000) *Research Methods in Education*, 5th edn. London: Routledge/Falmer.

Connolly, W. (1993) *The Terms of Political Discourse*, 3rd edn. Oxford: Blackwell.

Cousins, J. and Simon, M. (1996) The Nature and Impact of Policy-Induced Partnerships between Research and Practice Communities, *Educational Evaluation and Policy Analysis*, 18(3): 199–218.

Crosswaite, C. and Curtice, L. (1991) *Dissemination of Research for Health Promotion: A Literature Review*. Edinburgh: Research Unit in Health and Change, University of Edinburgh.

Crotty, M. (1998) *The Foundations of Social Research: Meaning and Perspective in the Research Process*. London: Sage.

Davies, B. (1987) Marriage and the construction of reality revisited: an exercise in rewriting social theory to include women's experience, *Educational Philosophy and Theory*, 19(1): 20–28.

Davies, B. (1996) *Power/Knowledge/Desire: Changing School Organisation and Management Practices*. Canberra: Department of Employment, Education and Youth Affairs.

Davies, B. (2000) *(In)scribing Body/Landscape Relations*. Walnut Creek: AltaMira Press.

Davies, P. (1999) What is Evidence-Based Education?, *British Journal of Educational Studies*, 47(2): 108–121.

De Landsheere, G. (1982) *Empirical Research in Education*. Paris: United Nations.

Delamont, S. (1990) *Sex Roles and the School*. London: Routledge.

Deleuze, G. (1995) *Negotiations*. New York: Columbia University Press.

Derrida, J. (1993) *Dissemination*. London: Athlone Press.

Dudley-Marling, C. (2001) School Trouble: A mother's burden, *Gender and Education*, 13(2): 183–197.

Edwards, R. (1990) Connecting Method and Epistemology: A white woman interviewing black women, *Women's Studies International Forum*, 13(5): 477–489.

Eichler, M. (1988) *Nonsexist Research Methods: A Practical Guide*. London: Unwin Hyman.

Einon, D. (1988) *Parenthood – the whole story*. London: Bloomsbury.

Ely, M. with Anzul, M., Friedman, T., Garner, D. and Steinmetz, A. (1991) *Doing Qualitative Research: Circles within Circles*. London: Falmer.

Epstein, A. (ed.) (1967) *The Craft of Social Anthropology*. London: Tavistock.

Eraut, M. (1985) Knowledge Creation and Knowledge Use in Professional Contexts, *Studies in Higher Education*, 10(2): 117–133.

Everton, T., Galton, M. and Pell, T. (2000) Teachers' Perspectives on Educational Research: Knowledge and Context, *Journal of Education for Teaching*, 26(2): 167–182.

Fauman, J. and Sharp, H. (1958) Presenting the Results of Social Research to the Public, *Public Opinion Quarterly*, 22(2): 107–115.

Finlayson, A. (1999) Language, in F. Ashe, A. Finalyson, M. Lloyd, I. MacKenzie, J. Martin and S. O'Neill, *Contemporary Social and Political Theory: An Introduction*. Buckingham: Open University Press.

Foucault, M. (1998) What is an author?, in J. Faubion (ed.) *Michel Foucault. Aesthetics*. New York: The New Press.

Foucault, M. (2000a) So is it important to think?, in J. Faubion (ed.) *Michel Foucault. Power*. New York: The New Press.

Foucault, M. (2000b) Truth and Power, in J. Faubion (ed.) *Michel Foucault. Power.* New York: The New Press.

Francis, B. (1998) *Power Plays: Primary School Children's Constructions of Gender, Power and Adult Work.* Stoke-on-Trent: Trentham Books.

Francis, B. (1999) Modernist reductionism or post-structuralist relativism: can we move on? An evaluation of the arguments in relation to feminist educational research, *Gender and Education*, 11(4): 381–394.

Francis, B. (2000) *Boys, Girls and Achievement: Addressing the Classroom Issues.* London: Routledge.

Francis, B. (2001) Beyond Postmodernism: feminist agency in educational research, in B. Francis and C. Skelton (eds) *Investigating Gender: Contemporary Perspectives in Education.* Buckingham: Open University Press.

Francis, B. (2001b) Commonality AND Difference? Attempts to escape from theoretical dualisms in emancipatory research in education, *International Sociology of Education Journal*, 11(2): 157–172.

Francis, B. (2002) Relativism, Realism and Feminism: an analysis of some theoretical tensions in research on gender identity, *Journal of Gender Studies*, 11(1): 39–54.

Franklin, S. (1969) *The European Peasantry: The Final Phase.* London: Methuen.

Freemantle, N. et al. (1994) Dissemination: Implementing the findings of research, *Health Libraries Review.* 11: 133–137.

Geertz, C. (2000) *Available Light: Anthropological Reflections on Philosophical topics.* Princeton: Princeton University Press.

Geiger, R. (1990) Organized Research Units: Their role in the development of university research, *Journal of Higher Education*, 61(1): 1–19.

Giddens, A. (1985) Time, Space and Regionalisation, in D. Gregory and J. Urry (eds) *Social Relations and Spatial Structures.* London: Macmillan.

Ginsburg, M., Adams, D., Clayton, T., Mantilla, M., Sylvester, J. and Wang, Y. (2000) The Politics of Linking Educational Research, Policy and Practice: The Case of Improving Educational Quality in Ghana, Guatemala and Mali, *International Journal of Community Studies*, XLI(1): 27–47.

Gordon, T. (1986) *Democracy in One School? Progressive Education and Restructuring.* London, New York and Philadelphia: Falmer Press.

Gordon, T. (1993) *Citizenship, Difference and Marginality in Schools: With Special Reference to Gender. A research proposal.* Helsinki: Academy of Finland.

Gordon, T. and Lahelma, E. (1996) 'School is like an Ants' Nest' – Spatiality and Embodiment in Schools, *Gender and Education*, 8(3): 301–10.

Gordon, T. and Lahelma, E. (2002) Becoming an Adult: Possibilities and Limitations – Dreams and Fears, *YOUNG*, 10(2): 2–18.

Gordon, T., Holland, J. and Lahelma, E. (2000) *Making Spaces: Citizenship and Difference in Schools.* London: Macmillan.

Gordon, T., Hynninen, P., Metso, T., Lahelma, E., Palmu, T. and Tolonen, T. (2000) Koulun arkea tutkimassa – Kokemuksia kollektiivisesta etnografiasta (Researching Everyday Life at School – Experiences from a Collective Ethnography), *Naistutkimus – kvinneforsking (Women's Studies)*, 13(1): 17–32.

Gordon, T., Lahelma, E. and Tolonen, T. (1995) 'Koulu on kuin . . .' metaforat fyysisen koulun analysoinnin välineenä ('School is like . . .' Using metaphors in analysing the physical school), *Nuorisotutkimus (Youth Studies)*, 3: 3–12.

Gordon, T., Lahelma, E., Hynninen, P., Metso, T., Palmu, T. and Tolonen, T. (1999) Learning the Routines: 'professionalization' of newcomers in secondary school, *International Journal of Qualitative Studies in Education*, (12)6: 689–706.

Green, C. (1988) *Babies! A Parent's Guide to Surviving (and Enjoying) Baby's First Year*. London: Simon and Schuster.

Green, C. (1992) *Toddler Taming: A Parent's Guide to the First Four Years*. London: Vermillion.

Griffiths, M. (1992) Making a Difference: Feminism, Postmodernism and the Methodology of Educational Research. ESRC Sponsored Seminar on Methodology and Epistemology in Educational Research, University of Liverpool, 22–24 June.

Griffiths, M. (1995) *Feminisms and the Self*. London: Routledge.

Griffiths, M. (1998) *Educational Research for Social Justice: Getting off the Fence*. Buckingham: Open University Press.

Grosz, E. (1990) Contemporary Theories of Power and Subjectivity, in S. Gunew (ed.) *Feminist Knowledge: Critique and Construct*, pp. 59–120. London: Routledge.

Grosz, E. (1995) *Volatile Bodies*. St Leonards: Allen and Unwin.

Guba, E. and Lincoln, Y. (1994) Competing Paradigms in Qualitative Research, in N. Denzin and Y. Lincoln (eds) *Handbook of Qualitative Research*, pp.105–117. Thousand Oaks (Calif): Sage.

Hammersley, M. (2000) Media Representation of Social Educational Research: The Case of a Review of Ethnic Minority Education, Paper presented at the British Educational Research Association Annual Conference, Cardiff University, September 7–10, www.leeds.ac.uk/educol/documnts/00001499.htm.

Harding, S. (1991) Feminism, Science and the Anti-Enlightenment Critiques, in L. Nicholson (ed.) *Feminism/Postmodernism*. London: Routledge.

Hardyment, C. (1995) *Perfect Parents*. Oxford: Oxford University Press.

Hargreaves, D. (1996) *Teaching as a Research Based Profession: Possibilities and Prospects*. London: Teacher Training Agency.

Hargreaves, D. (1997) In Defence of Research for Evidence-based Teaching: A rejoinder to Martyn Hammersley, *British Educational Research Journal*, 23(4): 405–419.

Hargreaves, D. (1999) The Knowledge-Creating School, *British Journal of Educational Studies*, 47(2): 122–144.

Harris, J. (1998) *The Nurture Assumption: Why children turn out the way they do*. London: Bloomsbury.

Havelock, R. (1969) *Planning for Innovation through Dissemination and Utilization of Knowledge*. Ann Arbour, MI: CRVSK, Institute for Social Research.

Havelock, R. (1973) *The Change Agent's Guide to Innovation in Education*. New Jersey: Educational Technology Publishers.

Health Education Authority (1994) *Birth to Five*. London: Health Education Authority.

HEQE (2001) A Guide to Dissemination, London, Higher Education Quality and Employability Division. www.dfeee.gov.uk/heqe/dissemguide.htm (accessed April 2001).

Hertz, R. and Imber, J. (eds) (1995) *Studying Elites Using Qualitative Methods*. Thousand Oaks, CA: Sage.

Heward, C. (1994) Academic snakes and merit ladders: reconceptualising the 'glass ceiling', *Gender and Education*, 63(3): 249–262.

Heward, C., Taylor, P. and Vickers, R. (1997) Gender, race and career success in the academic profession, *Journal of Further and Higher Education*, 21(2): 205–218.

Hey, V. (1999) Troubling the Auto/Biography of the Questions: re/thinking rapport and the politics of social class in feminist participant observation. Paper presented to the Gender & Education Second International Conference, University of Warwick, 29–31 April.

Hillage, J., Pearson, R., Anderson, A. and Tamkin, P. (1998) *Excellence in Research on Schools*, Research Report No 74. Sussex: Institute for Employment Studies.

Hood-Williams, J. (1998) Stories for Sexual Difference, *British Journal of Sociology of Education*, 18(1): 81–99.

Hooks, B. (1982) *Ain't I a Woman? Black Women and Feminism*. Boston, MA: Southend Press.

Hoskyns, C. (2000) The feminisation of politics? From Virginia Woolf to the network state. Inaugural lecture, Coventry University, 26 January.

Huberman, M. (1994) Research Utilization: The State of the Art, *Knowledge and Policy: International Journal of Knowledge Transfer and Utilization*, 7(4): 13–33.

Hughes, C. (2000) Learning to be intellectually insecure: the dis/empowering effects of reflexive practice, *International Journal of Social Research Methodology*, 1(4): 281–296.

Hughes, C. (2002a) *Key Concepts in Feminist Theory and Research*. London: Sage.

Hughes, C. (2002b) *Women's Contemporary Lives: Within and Beyond the Mirror*. London: Routledge.

Huizer G. and Mannheim B. (eds) (1979) *The Politics of Anthropology: From Colonialism and Sexism to a View from Below*. The Hague: Mouton.

Issit, M. (2002) Taking the Experience Route: Accrediting Competence through Feminism and Critical Reflective Practice. Unpublished PhD thesis, Manchester Metropolitan University, Manchester.

Johnson, S. (1995) Women in Transition: A study of the experiences of women beginning programmes of professional higher education. Paper presented to the European Conference on Educational Research, University of Bath, 14–17 September.

Jones, A. (1997) Teaching post-structuralist feminist theory in education: student resistances, *Gender & Education*, 9(3): 261–269.

Katz, E., Levin, M. and Hamilton, H. (1963) Traditions of Research on the Diffusion of Innovation, *American Sociological Review*, 28(2): 237–252.

Kirst, M. (2000) Bridging Education Research and Education Policy Making, *Oxford Review of Education*, 26(3, 4): 379–391.

Knott, J. and Wildavsky, A. (1991) If dissemination is the solution, what is the problem?, in D. Anderson and B. Biddle (eds) *Knowledge for Policy: Improving Education through Research*. London: Falmer Press.

Lahelma, E. and Gordon, T. (1997) First Day in Secondary School: Learning to be a 'Professional Pupil', *Educational Research and Evaluation*, 3(2): 119–139.

Lahelma, E. and Gordon, T. (forthcoming) *Koulun arki: Tutkijat yläasteella (Everyday Life at School: Researchers in Secondary School)*. Helsinki: City of Helsinki Education Office.

Lavender, P. (2000) Lifelong Learning and the Social Equity Agenda: Context and Challenges, in *Lifelong Learning Research and the Social Equity Agenda*, ESRC Seminar Series 1999–2000. Leeds: School of Continuing Education, University of Leeds.

Laws, C. and Davies, B. (2000) Poststructuralist theory in practice: working with 'behaviourally disturbed' children. *International Journal of Qualitative Studies in Education*, 13(3): 205–21.

Leach, P. (1997) *Your Baby and Child: The Essential Guide for Every Parent*. Middlesex: Penguin Books.

Lewando Hundt, G. (2000) Multiple Scripts and Contested Discourse in Disseminating Research Findings, *Social Policy and Administration*, 34(4): 419–433.

Lewis, S. (1991) Motherhood and employment: the impact of organisational and social values, in A. Phoenix, A. Woollett and E. Lloyd (eds) *Motherhood: Meanings, Practices and Ideologies*. London: Sage.

Lloyd, B. and Duveen, G. (1992) *Gender Identities and Education: The impact of starting school*. Hemel Hempstead: Harvester Press.

Lomax, P. (1999) Working Together for Educative Community through Research, *British Educational Research Journal*, 25(1): 5–21.

Lynch, K. (1999) Equality studies, the academy and the role of research in emancipatory social change, *The Economic and Social Review*, 30(1).

Maguire, P. (1987) *Doing Participatory Action Research: A Feminist Approach*. Massachusetts: Centre for International Education.

Mahony, D. (1994) Government and the New Universities: The 'New Mutuality' in Australian Higher Education – a National Case Study, *Journal of Higher Education*, 65(2): 123–146.

Mann, C. (2002) Men accelerate – women accumulate, *Science and Social Affairs*, April.

Marsh, C. (1986) Dissemination strategies and tactics, *British Journal of Educational Research*, 34(2): 182–197.

Marshall, H. (1991) The social construction of motherhood: an analysis of childcare and parenting manuals, in A. Phoenix, A. Woollett and E. Lloyd (eds) *Motherhood: Meanings, Practices and Ideologies*. London: Sage.

Massey, D. (2001) Blurring the binaries? High tech in Cambridge, in C. Paechter, M. Preedy, D. Scott and J. Soler (eds) *Knowledge, Power and Learning*. London: Paul Chapman Publishing.

Maynard, M. (1994) Methods, Practice and Epistemology: The Debate About Feminism and Research, in M. Maynard and J. Purvis (eds) *Researching Women's Lives from a Feminist Perspective*. London: Taylor and Francis.

Maynard, M. and Purvis, J. (eds) (1994) *Researching Women's Lives from a Feminist Perspective*. London: Taylor and Francis.

Mbilinyi, M. (1982) My experience as a woman activist and researcher in a project with peasant women, in M. Mies (ed.) *Fighting on Two Fronts: Women's Struggles and Research*. The Hague: Institute of Social Studies.

Mbilinyi, M. (1982) The unity of struggle and research: the case of peasant women in W. Bagamoyo, Tanzania, in M. Mies (ed.) *Fighting on Two Fronts: Women's Struggles and research*. The Hague: Institute of Social Studies.

McDevitt, D. (2001) How Effective is the Cascade as a Method for Disseminating

Ideas? A Case Study in Botswana, *International Journal of Educational Development*, 18(5): 425–428.

McIntyre, J. and Wickert, R. (2000) The Negotiated Management of Meanings: Research for Policy, in J. Garrick and C. Rhodes (eds) *Research and Knowledge at Work: Perspectives, Case Studies and Innovative Strategies*. London: Routledge.

McKernan, J. (1991) *Curriculum Action Research: A Handbook of Methods and Resources for the Reflective Practitioner*, 2nd edn. London: Kogan Page.

McMillan, J. and Schumacher, S. (1989) *Research in Education: A Conceptual Introduction*. London: Harper Collins.

Mendras, H. (1970) *The Vanishing Peasants: Innovation and Change in French Agriculture*. London: MIT Press.

Mies, M. (1983) Towards a methodology for feminist research, in G. Bowles and R. Duelli-Klein (eds) *Theories of Women's Studies*. London: Routledge.

Miller, D. (1997) How infants grow mothers in North London, *Theory, Culture and Society*, 14(4): 67–88.

Mirza, H. (ed.) (1997) *Black British Feminism*. London: Routledge.

Mirza, M. (1995) Some Ethical Dilemmas in Fieldwork: feminist and anti-racist methodologies, in M. Griffiths and B. Troyna (eds) *Anti-Racism, Culture and Social Justice in Education*. Stoke-on-Trent: Trentham Books.

Morley, D. (1997) Theoretical orthodoxies: Textualism, constructivism and the New Ethnography in Cultural Studies, in M. Ferguson and P. Golding (eds) *Cultural Studies in Question*. Sage: London.

Morrison, T. (1993) *Playing in the Dark: Whiteness and the Literary Imagination*. Cambridge, MA: Harvard University Press.

Murphy, E. and Dingwall, R. (2001) The Ethics of Ethnography, in P. Atkinson, A. Coffey, S. Delamont, J. Lofland and L. Lofland (eds) *Handbook of Ethnography*. London, Thousand Oaks, New Delhi: Sage.

NERF (2000) *The Impact of Educational Research on Policy and Practice*. National Educational Research Forum Sub-Group Report, December 2000. www.nerf-org.uk.

Norris, C. (2000) Post-modernism: a guide for the perplexed, in G. Browning, A. Halcli and F. Webster (eds) *Understanding Contemporary Society: Theories of the Present*, pp.25–45. London: Sage.

Oakley, A. (2002) Social Science and Evidence-based Everything: the case of education, *Educational Review*, 54(3): 277–286.

Odendahl, T. and Shaw, A. (2002) Interviewing elites, in Gubrium, J. and Holstein, J. (eds) *Handbook of Interview Research*, pp.299–316. Thousand Oaks, CA: Sage.

Organisation for Economic Cooperation and Development (1995) *Educational Research and Development: Trends, Issues and Challenges*. Paris: OECD.

Ostrander, S. (1995) 'Surely you're not in this just to be helpful': Access, rapport and interviews in three studies of elites', in R. Hertz and J. Imber (eds) *Studying Elites Using Qualitative Methods*, pp.133–151. Thousand Oaks, CA: Sage.

Ozga, J. (2000) *Policy Research In Educational Settings*. Buckingham: Open University Press.

Paechter, C. (1998) *Educating the Other: Gender, Power and Schooling*. London: Falmer Press.

Parker, I. (1992) *Discourse Dynamics: Critical Analysis for Social and Individual Psychology*. London: Routledge.

Pattman, R., Phoneix, A. and Frosh, S. (1998) Lads, machos and others: developing 'boy-centred' research, *Journal of Youth Studies*, 1: 125–142.

Paulsen, M. and Feldman, K. (1995) Towards a Reconceptualization of Scholarship: A human action system with functional imperatives, *Journal of Higher Education*, 66(6): 615–640.

Phoenix, A. (1987) Theories of Gender and Black Families, in G. Weiner and M. Arnot (eds) *Gender Under Scrutiny*. London: Hutchinson.

Pocock, D. (1975) *Understanding Social Anthropology*. London: Hodder and Stoughton.

Probyn, E. (1993) *Sexing the Self: Gendered Positions in Cultural Studies*. London: Routledge.

Raddon, A. (2001a) *Research Dissemination in Education: A Literature Review*. Coventry: Department of Continuing Education, University of Warwick.

Raddon, A. (2001b) (M)others in the academy: positioned and positioning within discourses of the 'successful academic' and the 'good mother'. Paper presented to the Third International Conference of Gender and Education: The Politics of Gender and Education, Institute of Education, University of London, April.

Raphael-Reed, L. (2001) Re-searching, re-finding, re-making: Exploring the unconscious as a pedagogic and research practice, in B. Francis and C. Skelton (eds) *Investigating Gender: Contemporary Perspectives in Education*. Buckingham: Open University Press.

Reay, D. (1998) *Class Work: Mothers' Involvement in Their Children's Primary Schooling*. London: UCL Press.

Reay, D. (2000) 'Dim dross': marginalised women both inside and outside the academy, *Women's Studies International Forum*, 23(1): 13–21.

Renzetti, C. and Lee, R. (eds) (1993) *Researching Sensitive Topics*. Newbury Park, CA: Sage.

Riquarts, K. and Hansen, K. (1998) Collaboration among teachers, researchers and in-service trainers to develop an integrated science curriculum, *Journal of Curriculum Studies*, 30(6): 661–676.

Roman, L. (1993) Double Exposure: The Politics of Feminist Materialist Ethnography, *Educational Theory*, 43(3): 279–308.

Rose, N. (1999) *Powers of Freedom*. Cambridge: Cambridge University Press.

Rudduck, J. (1973) Dissemination in practice, *Cambridge Journal of Education*, 3(3): 143–158.

Rudduck, J. and Kelly, P. (1976) *The Dissemination of Curriculum Development: Current Trends*. Windsor: NFER.

Said, E. (1978) *Orientalism*. London: Routledge Kegan Paul.

Said, E. with photographs by Mohr, J. (1986) *After the Last Sky*. London: Faber and Faber.

Sargisson, L. (1996) *Contemporary Feminist Utopianism*. London: Routledge.

Sax, G. (1979) *Foundations of Educational Research*. Englewood Cliffs, New Jersey: Prentice-Hall Inc.

Schon, D. (ed.) (1991) *The Reflective Turn*. New York: Teachers College Press.

Schuller, T. (1996) The Impact of Research, in R. Taylor and D. Watson (eds) *From Continuing Education to Lifelong Learning: A Review of Universities Association for Continuing Education Strategy and Objectives*, Occasional Paper No. 20. London: UACE.

Seashore Louis, S. (1994) Improving Urban and Disadvantaged Schools, *Knowledge and Policy: International Journal of Knowledge Transfer and Utilization*, 7(4): 34–54.

Seidman, I. (1991) *Interviewing as Qualitative Research*. Columbia University: Teachers College Press.

Shotton, J. (1989) *No Master High or Low: Libertarian Education and Schooling in Britain 1890–1990*. Bristol: Libertarian Education.

Sikes, P. (1997) *Parents Who Teach: Stories from Home and from School*. London: Cassell.

Skeggs, B. (1994) Situating the Production of Feminist Methodology, in M. Maynard and J. Purvis (eds) *Researching Women's Lives from a Feminist Perspective*. London: Taylor and Francis.

Skeggs, B. (2001) Feminist Ethnography, in P. Atkinson, A. Coffey, S. Delamont, J. Lofland and L. Lofland (eds) *Handbook of Ethnography*. London: Sage.

Slim, H. and Thompson, P. (1993) *Listening for a Change: Oral Testimony and Development*. London: Panos.

Smith, L. (1999) *Decolonizing Methodologies: Research and Indigenous Peoples*. London: Zed Books.

Smith, V. (2001) Ethnographies of Work and the Work of Ethnographers, in P. Atkinson, A. Coffey, S. Delamont, J. Lofland and L. Lofland (eds) *Handbook of Ethnography*. London: Sage.

Soper, K. (1990) *Troubled Pleasures*. London: Verso.

Spivak, G. (1999) *A Critique of Postcolonial Reason*. Cambridge (Mass): Harvard University Press.

Spivak, G. and Gunew S. (1989) Questions of multiculturalism, in M. Broe and A. Ingram (eds) *Women's Writing in Exile*. London: Chapel Hill.

Stacey, J. (1988) Can there be a feminist ethnography?, *Women's Studies International Forum*, 11(1): 21–27.

Stacey, J. (1990) *Brave New Families: Stories of Domestic Upheaval in Late Twentieth Century*. New York: Basic Books.

Stahler, G. and Tash, W. (1994) Centers and Institutes in the Research University: Issues, Problems and Prospects, *Journal of Higher Education*, 65(5): 540–554.

Stanley, L. and Wise, S. (1993) *Breaking Out Again: Feminist Ontology and Epistemology*. London: Sage.

Stokking, K. (1994) Dissemination and Diffusion of Knowledge and Innovation, in T. Husen and T. Postlethwaite (1994) *The International Encyclopedia of Education*, Vol. 3, 2nd edn. Oxford: Elsevier.

Tanesini, A. (1994) Whose Language?, in K. Lennon and M. Whitford (eds) *Knowing the Difference: Feminist Perspectives in Epistemology*. London: Routledge.

Tight, M. (1988) *Academic Freedom and Responsibility*. Milton Keynes: Open University Press/SRHE.

Tolonen, T. (2001) *Nuorten kulttuurit koulussa: Ääni, tila ja sukupuolten arkiset järjestykset (Voice, Space and Gender in Youth Cultures at School)*. Helsinki: Gaudeamus.

Tooley, J. with Darby, D. (1988) *Education Research: A Critique*. London: Office for Standards in Education.

Van Maanen, J. (1988) *Tales of the Field: On Writing Ethnography.* Chicago: University of Chicago Press.

Walker, J. (1988) The way men act: dominant and subordinate male cultures in an inner-city school, *British Journal of Sociology of Education,* 9(1): 3–18.

Walkerdine, V. and Lucey, H. (1989) *Democracy in the Kitchen.* London: Virago.

Walsh, V. (2001) From tangle to web: life history as feminist process. Paper presented at Department of Continuing Education, University of Warwick, 15 February.

Watkins, J. (1994) A Postmodern Critical Theory of Research Use, *Knowledge and Policy: International Journal of Knowledge Transfer and Utilization,* 7(4): 55–77.

Weedon, C. (1999) *Feminism, Theory and the Politics of Difference.* Oxford: Blackwell.

Weiner, G. (1998) Scholarship, Disciplinary Hegemony and Power in Academic Publishing. Paper presented to the European Conference for Educational Research, University of Ljubljana, Slovenia, September 17–20.

Weiss, C. (ed.) (1977) *Using Social Research in Public Policy Making.* Lexington, MA: Lexington Books.

Weiss, C. (1982) Policy Research in the Context of Diffuse Decision Making, *Journal of Higher Education,* 53(6): 619–639.

Wellin, C. and Fine, G. (2001) Ethnography as Work: Career Socialisation, Settings and Problems, in P. Atkinson, A. Coffey, S. Delamont, J. Lofland and L. Lofland (eds) *Handbook of Ethnography.* London: Sage.

Wisker, G. (2000) *Post-colonial and African American Women's Writing: A Critical Introduction.* Basingstoke: MacMillan.

Woodward, K. (ed.) (1997) *Identity and Difference.* London: Sage/Open University Press.

Yudice, G. (1988) Marginality and the Ethics of Survival, in A. Ross (ed.) *Universal Abandon? The Politics of Postmodernism.* Edinburgh: Edinburgh University Press.

Zuzovsky, R. (1994) Utilization of Research Findings: A Matter of Research Tradition, *Knowledge and Policy: International Journal of Knowledge Transfer and Utilization,* 7(4): 78–93.

Index

ETHNOGRAPHY FOR EDUCATION

Christopher Pole and Marlene Morrison

Ethnography is a distinctive approach for educational research. The authors argue that the last decade has seen ethnography come of age, not only as a way of doing research, but also as a way of theorizing and making sense of the world. Their approach is concerned with ethnography as process and ethnography as product. This critical celebration of ethnography explores what it can achieve in educational research.

The book features:

- Thorough discussion of definitions of ethnography and its potential for use within educational research
- Critical introductions to the principal approaches to ethnography
- Discussions of data analysis and representation and of the challenges facing ethnography
- Use of educational examples from real research projects throughout.

The book offers a distinctive contribution to the literature of ethnography, taking readers beyond a simplistic "how to" approach towards an understanding of the wider contribution ethnography can make to our understanding of educational processes.

Ethnography for Education is of value to final-year undergraduates and postgraduates in education and social science disciplines, as well as education professionals engaged in practice-based research.

Contents
Defining ethnography – Doing ethnography: primary sources – Doing ethnography: secondary sources – Analysing ethnographic data – Using ethnography – Representing ethnography – Conclusions and challenges – References – Index.

160pp   0 335 20600 X (Paperback)   0 335 20601 8 (Hardback)

NARRATIVES AND FICTIONS IN EDUCATIONAL RESEARCH

Peter Clough

In this bold and very important work, Peter Clough shows how the truths about educational issues can be told using fictional devices. This work legitimates the narrative turn in the human disciplines. He shows educational researchers how narrative inquiry can be used for progressive moral and political purposes.

Norman K. Denzin, University of Illinois at Urbana-Champaign

This compelling book takes a fresh approach to educational research, considering the role and use of literary and ethnographic approaches. There is growing interest in the use of narrative and fictional methods and this book sets out to:

- locate narrative and fictional methods within the traditions of education research;
- exemplify the use of narrative in studies of educational and social settings;
- explain the processes of composing narrative and fictional research.

A distinctive feature of the book is the inclusion of five 'fictional' stories which demonstrate the use of narrative in reporting research. Detailed discussion of these five stories shows how they were created from actual events and the varied role of the author in their creation. The methodological implications of such an approach are considered along with its potential merits and difficulties and its possible uses.

Contents
Preface – The man with the blue guitar – Stories from educational research: an introduction – The map is not the terrain – Klaus – Molly – Rob – Bev – Lolly (the final word) – Hard to tell: the readings of the stories – Narratives of educational practice – To the things themselves – References – Index.

128pp   0 335 20791 X (Paperback)   0 335 20792 8 (Hardback)

LIFE HISTORY RESEARCH IN EDUCATIONAL SETTINGS
LEARNING FROM LIVES

Ivor Goodson and Pat Sikes

It has long been recognized that life history method has a great deal to offer to those engaged in social research. Indeed, right from the start of the twentieth century, eminent sociologists such as W.I. Thomas, C. Wright Mills and Hubert Blumer have suggested that it is the best, the perfect, approach for studying any aspect of social life. In recent years, life history has become increasingly popular with researchers investigating educational topics of all kinds, including: teachers' perceptions and experiences of different areas of their lives and careers; curriculum and subject development; pedagogical practice; and managerial concerns. *Life History Research in Educational Settings* sets out to explore and consider the various reasons for this popularity and makes the case that the approach has a major and unique contribution to make to understandings of schools, schooling and educational experience, however characterized. The book draws extensively on examples of life history research in order to illustrate theoretical, methodological, ethical and practical issues.

Contents

144pp   0 335 20713 8 (Paperback)   0 335 20714 6 (Hardback)